Other Translations by Thomas Cleary

TAOISM

The Inner Teachings of Taoism
Understanding Reality: A Taoist Alchemical Classic
Awakening to the Tao
The Art of War
Immortal Sisters
Mastering the Art of War

I CHING STUDIES

The Taoist I Ching
The Buddhist I Ching
I Ching: The Tao of Organization
I Ching Mandalas

BUDDHISM

The Blue Cliff Record
The Original Face
Timeless Spring
Shobogenzo: Zen Essays by Dōgen
Entry into the Inconceivable
The Flower Ornament Scripture
Zen Lessons: The Art of Leadership
Entry into the Realm of Reality
Zen Essence

Transmission of Light

{Denkoroku}

Zen in the Art of Enlightenment

By Zen Master Keizan

Translated and with an Introduction
by Thomas Cleary

North Point Press
San Francisco   1990

LIBRARY OF CONGRESS
CATALOGING IN PUBLICATION DATA
Keizan, 1268–1325.
   [Denkōroku. English]
   Transmission of light : Zen in the art of enlighten-
ment / by Keizan ; translated and with an introduc-
tion by Thomas Cleary.
    p.   cm.
   Translation of: Denkōroku.
   ISBN 0-86547-429-X. —ISBN 0-86547-433-8 (pbk.)
   1. Sōtōshū—Early works to 1800.   2. Priests,
Zen—Biography—Early works to 1800.
   I. Title.
BQ9415.K4513   1990
294.3'927—dc20   89-28491

North Point Press
850 Talbot Avenue
Berkeley, California
94706

Contents

Introduction

Transmission of Light is one of the major classics of Japanese Zen Buddhism. Ostensibly a collection of stories about fifty-three Buddhist illuminates from India, China, and Japan, in reality it is a book of instruction in the art of satori—Zen enlightenment. Satori is the essential initiatory experience of Zen Buddhism, the beginning of true Zen realization, and *Transmission of Light* is the most thorough guide to satori in the entire Japanese Zen canon. Using its format of tales about the awakenings of fifty-three successive generations of masters, *Transmission of Light* illustrates quintessential techniques for realization of satori, showing how this experience transcends time, history, culture, race, gender, personality, and social status.

Zen writings commonly refer to satori as realization of the "original mind" as it is in itself, the universal ground of consciousness, concealed beneath the temporal conditioning that forces people to experience life through outlooks arbitrarily limited by their cultural, social, and personal histories. This realization is considered the essential initiatory experience of Zen in that it allows the individual access to a range of mental potential beyond the limitations of outlook defined by ordinary processes of acculturation, socialization, and education. In classical Taoism, the Chinese forerunner of Zen, this is known as "the use of the unused."

Satori is therefore said to be the key to inner freedom and independence, the door to higher knowledge, realized by all enlightened people: in the words of Dogen, one of the founders of Zen in Japan, "As each of them attained escape from the shell, they were unencumbered by previous views and understandings, and what had long been unclear suddenly became apparent." Thus while satori, as radical liberation from needless constraints of inculcated worldviews, is often spoken of in dramatic terms as a shattering experience, in Zen it is understood not as destructive but essentially constructive—in the sense that it is the threshold of conscious access to the inherent potential for greater completeness and fuller life that lies fallow in the ordinary mind.

Many of the metaphors traditionally used for satori revolve around images of death, for it frees the individual from the identification of personality with self: "Let go over a sheer cliff," the Zen proverb says. "Die completely and then come back to life—after that no one can deceive you." The new life after satori is richer for having let go of circumstantially ingrained attachments, biases, and blind spots that close minds into tunnel visions of life and make individuals, groups, and masses vulnerable to manipulation. "See the playing of the puppets on the stage," wrote an ancient Zen master. "All along there is someone inside pulling the strings." Without satori, people are like puppets on the stage; on awakening, they realize who is pulling the strings.

There are, nevertheless, definite drawbacks associated with specific reactions to the Zen teaching of satori. Most of these drawbacks, well documented throughout Zen literature, are related in some way to responses people manifest to the emphasis traditionally placed on satori in Zen teaching. One such problem is neglect of adequate preparation due to eagerness for quick results: "No one knows the sweating horses of the past; they only want to talk over the achievement that crowns the age." This attitude may prevent satori altogether, may induce the person in this state to mistake exciting states for satori, or make the enthusiast unable to sustain an occasional intimation or glimpse of the experience: "Everything gained in battle is ruined by celebrating."

This last quotation, from the sayings of a Chinese Zen master, also alludes to another typical shortcoming: failure to consummate satori by carelessness in its aftermath. Satori is not the end of Zen; it is more properly the true beginning. Those who stop here are traditionally said to have "gained a little and considered it enough." Another Zen proverb refers to this defect: "The level ground is littered with skulls; the experts are those who pass through the forest of thorns."

A classical master explains this point in more detail: "Though beginners may have conditionally attained an instantaneous realization of inherent noumenon, there are still the habit energies of time immemorial that they cannot clear away all at once. It is necessary to teach them to clean out their present conditioned stream of consciousness." A later Zen master notes that immature satori can itself be made an object of attachment (one of the notorious dangers of cultic emphasis on peak experience and celebration of its attainment), a process which then blocks the aspirant from deeper realization: "Lesser enlightenment after all turns out to be a hindrance to greater enlightenment. If you give up lesser enlightenments and don't cling to them, greater enlightenment will surely be realized. If you grasp little enlightenment and don't relinquish it, great enlightenment will surely be ignored. This is like someone so greedy for a little profit that he doesn't get a big profit. If he doesn't cling greedily to a little profit, great profit will eventually be realized; if he accumulates small profits, eventually it will amount to great profit."

When stress is placed on satori (and stress is the word) to the extent that seekers lose sight of these traditional caveats, it also may happen that extreme methods acting upon eagerly unprepared minds result in exhaustion, nervous breakdown, or even derangement. Such problems are said to occur because of imbalance—failure to understand all aspects of Zen practice and experience in context as part of a coherent whole. And this is ordinarily due to greed disguised as spirituality, not to any failure of genuine Zen technical literature to warn practitioners about inexpert or improper manipulation of mind. While physical and mental problems resulting from fragmentary and misapplied Zen techniques are said to heal if the practices are abandoned, there is continuing danger to unwary seekers when mental exhaustion, nervous overload, and other altered states of consciousness are mistaken for spiritual progress, or for satori itself.

The present work, *Transmission of Light*, one of the most prestigious texts of Japanese Zen, is perhaps unparalleled in its emphasis on the need for real satori. Zen history shows that this essential gnosis is easily lost in the course of tradition, and there has never been, according to overall Buddhist teaching, a standard formula for enlightenment. Therefore a very direct teaching of satori appears throughout the Zen teaching, but projected in the context of certain basic understandings.

There are many schools of Buddhism, each appealing to people of certain mentalities. Within the Zen tradition there are different schools as well, each with its characteristic mood. *Transmission of Light* is an early classic of the Japanese Soto school of Zen, which is characterized by the disguises it uses to clothe the teaching of satori. Sometimes it is so heavily veiled that whole sects of Soto Zen followers have at times come to believe there is no satori in their teaching. Nevertheless, satori teaching is part of the original teaching of Soto Zen, and in this it is no different from Rinzai Zen, the other major Japanese school.

Changlu Lin, an eleventh-generation master of one of the Chinese Soto schools, gives a talk on satori in terms similar to those encountered in *Transmission of Light*: "The source of the school is apart from conscious thought and perception; the message transcends past, future, and present. Being apart from conscious thought and perception, in classifying myriad species no difference is seen; transcending time, nothing anywhere afflicts you anymore. Immediately not transgressing, ultimately not depending, awakening is before the appearance of signs, function is where training doesn't reach. In daily life one shouldn't hesitate—in the interval of hesitation one loses contact."

Similar instructions are given by Fawei, another Chinese Soto master, who also emphasizes the importance of the aftermath: "The spiritual body has no characteristics—it cannot be sought through sound. The marvelous path has no words—it cannot be understood through writings. Even if you transcend Buddhas and Zen masters, you still fall into gradation; even if you speak of the marvelous and mysterious, in the end it sticks to your teeth. You should be unaffected by training, not leaving a trace of form, a withered tree on a frigid cliff, without any moisture left, a phantom, a wooden horse, all emotional consciousness empty—only then can you enter the marketplace with open hands, operating freely in the midst of all kinds of people and situations. As it is said, 'Don't linger in the land of detachment; come back to the misty bank and lie on the cold sand.' "

Zen lore abounds with allusions to the transcendental nature of satori, but this also means transcending the inner silence used as means of access to satori and consummating the experience by "return" to the ordinary world. This is particularly true of the Chinese Soto schools and the original Japanese Soto school under the tutelage of Zen master Dogen. In the words of Touzi, a seventh-generation Chinese Soto master, "Where you don't fall into vacant stillness, the way back is more marvelous."

Hongzhi, a tenth-generation Chinese Soto master often quoted in Dogen's sayings, similarly stressed the equal importance of both phases—transcendence and reintegration: "If the host does not know there is a guest, there is no way to respond to the world; if a guest does not know there is a host, there is no vision beyond material sense." When asked how to achieve thoroughgoing penetration, Hongzhi said: "When you are open and clean, undefiled, 'the clear sky is cloudless, there is no breeze on the autumn waters.' When you are pure and plain, master of yourself, 'the jade vase is free of dust, there is no dirt on the ice mirror.' But when you reach such a state, you should go on to 'borrow light to set up facilities, borrow a road to pass through.' Merge your mind with cosmic space, integrate your actions with myriad forms."

As one of the founders of Zen in Japan, the thirteenth-century master Dogen naturally placed emphasis on satori: "Explanation of the teaching must be appropriate to the time and situation. If it is not appropriate to the time, it is all untimely talk. Is there any in accord with the time? (Silence.) Expounding Zen in Japan must be before the prehistoric Buddhas, on the other side of the King of Emptiness—not in the neighborhood of ancient Chinese teachers." In the language of Zen, "before the prehistoric Buddhas" and "on the other side of the King of Emptiness" are both expressions for satori. In plain terms, therefore, Dogen's statement means that the authentic founding of Zen teaching calls for direct experience of satori, not mere imitation of past formulations in a different cultural milieu.

In his most popular work on meditation, Dogen gives instructions for realization of satori through what he calls "the essential art of zazen." Dogen's masterwork *Shobogenzo* explicitly shows that zazen, which may be provisionally if imprecisely translated as "sitting meditation," was a highly fluid and complex affair in Dogen's school. But his description of the "essential art" refers to a basic technique common not only to all Zen schools but to all of the five major schools of Buddhism in China: "You should stop the intellectual practice of pursuing words, and learn the stepping back of 'turning the light around and looking inward.' Mind and body will naturally drop off, and the 'original face' will appear." In characteristic Zen fashion, Dogen also used an ancient story for an abstract model of the exercise, calling it "thinking of what does not think."

While he gave out a number of such basic exercises in his popular teaching, in his masterwork Dogen generally veiled references to initiatory satori experience. One reason for this caution was that he was particularly adamant in his emphasis on the need to transcend consciousness of the experience and attend to the aftermath. Thus the risk of arousing emotional enthusiasm about satori was no doubt too great, considering the obstacles it could put in the way of the task of his teaching cycle.

Without satori and knowledge of the other schools Dogen mastered, it is not always easy to see this element precisely in much of his work. But Dogen is very explicit on the matter of his cycle of emphasis in the popular treatise on zazen quoted above: "Even if one can boast of understanding, is rich in enlightenment, gains a glimpse of penetrating knowledge, attains the Way, clarifies the mind, and becomes very high spirited, nevertheless even though one roams freely within the bounds of initiatory experience, one may lack the living road of manifestation in being." Similarly, in another popular essay he wrote: "There is ceasing the traces of enlightenment, which causes one to forever leave the traces of enlightenment which is cessation."

Dogen's great emphasis on post-satori maturation is completely in accord with Zen tradition, but the historical circumstances of his teaching no doubt contributed to the abundance of references to this theme found in his works. He lived in a time when many outstanding Buddhists were breaking away from the old schools, sensing that something was missing in their teaching and practice. Almost all of Dogen's original students had been followers of a native Japanese Zen school that had restored the teaching of satori to Buddhism, and the dramatic effect this teaching produced naturally resulted in enormous enthusiasm for this experience as the magic key or missing link.

Unfortunately, as has been documented throughout most of the history of Zen, practitioners of this and other new Zen schools were evidently tempted to regard satori as the end rather than a beginning of Zen practice, thus lapsing into the complacency suggested by the proverb cited earlier: "the level ground is littered with skulls." When Dogen's work is seen through this eye, his repeated references to this problem and its resolution, often concealed within the structure of what seem to be philosophical disquisitions, become clearly apparent for what they are: abstract representations of this central issue of Zen praxis.

This critical point in the Zen mental revolution is illustrated elegantly in Dogen's essay "The Dragon Howl," which is based on an ancient meditation story. A student asked a Zen master, "Is there a dragon howl in a dead tree?" The master said, "I say there is a lion roar in a skull." Here the "dead tree" and the "skull" represent the "great death" of Zen, the liberation of mind from the mesmeric grip of its creations, the opening of satori; whereas the "dragon howl" and the "lion roar" stand for the "great function," the expanded access of potential that the Zen "death" makes possible.

In this essay, Dogen takes great pains to distinguish the "great death" from hypnosis-induced apathy, suppression, quietism, or attachment to detachment: "Talk about the dead tree and dead ashes is originally a deviant teaching, but the dead tree spoken of by deviants and the dead tree spoken of by the enlightened are very different. Although deviants talk about the dead tree, they do not know the dead tree, much less hear the dragon howl. Deviants think the dead tree is dead wood, and practice as if there is no more spring for it."

Insisting on the interdependence of Zen "death" and renewal, Dogen goes on to say: "The leaves spread based on the root—this is called the enlightened ones; root and branch must return to the source—this is penetrating study." While he notes that the greater potential is inherent and never really lost even when unrealized—"If it is not a dead tree, it does not lose the dragon howl"—nevertheless he affirms that satori is necessary for the actualization of this potential—"As long as it is not a dead tree, it does not make the dragon howl."

The most outstanding characteristic of Dogen's masterwork *Shobogenzo* is his emphasis on the dangers of confusing satori with altered states of mind, or with simple detachment from states of mind, and the dangers of overemphasizing the peak experience of satori at the expense of aftermath development. In contrast to this, the most outstanding characteristic of *Transmission of Light*, which ranks with Dogen's work as a major classic of Soto Zen, is its extremely penetrating analysis of the process of satori. There is, to be sure, a great deal more to be found in *Transmission of Light*, but insistence on the necessity of genuine satori and the thoroughly transcendent nature of the experience emerges in so many guises, chapter after chapter, that it becomes the overriding theme of the whole work, making *Transmission of Light* the classic statement of satori practice.

Transmisson of Light is attributed to Zen master Keizan (1268–1325), a great fourth-generation master of Dogen's school. He was the first to spread Soto Zen teaching to a wide audience and is formally ranked by Japanese Soto tradition in a position of honor second only to the founder Dogen himself. Recent scholarly investigations have cast doubt on the authorship of *Transmission of Light*, but these need not concern us here—not only because of the speciousness of some of the arguments advanced against the traditional attribution, but more importantly because the first principle of universalist Buddhist hermeneutics is to "rely on the truth, not the personality."

It seems reasonable to assume that the author was a representative of the Soto school of Zen, and it seems clear that the author was knowledgeable about the main satori methods employed in Chinese Zen of the Song dynasty (960–1278). The Soto origin of the text is important only insofar as it testifies to the falsehood of certain common distortions and myths about Soto Zen fostered by sectarian cultists. The technical expertise it displays, on the other hand, is of transhistorical importance in that it provides genuine guidance in the matter of attaining and authenticating true satori experience. If people attain real satori, sectarian cultism is not their worry and distinguishing myth from reality is not their problem.

Because of the tremendous confusion and uncertainty attending critical study of the early history of Japanese Soto Zen and the patterns of circulation of Dogen's work, it is not necessarily possible to ascertain precise historical reasons for the enormous effort made by the author of *Transmission of Light* to reestablish the prime importance of satori and debunk sectarian quirks. There is no question, however, that a schism occurred within Soto Zen shortly after Dogen's passing and that a number of disputes erupted over the abbacy of the monastery Dogen founded.

It is not certain when use of Dogen's masterwork fell into abeyance, but it is extremely difficult to find any reference to it in Soto works after the third generation, and it seems to disappear from active Soto teaching until the late seventeenth or early eighteenth century. Furthermore, the succession disputes and sectarian schism that took place in the third to fourth generation had already demonstrated blatant disregard for some of Dogen's most fundamental teachings—basic principles of Buddhism emphasized not only in his masterwork and regular talks but also in his early groundwork lectures.

In any case, *Transmission of Light* is very forthright in acknowledging degeneration in the Soto Zen of its time. It openly attacks monastic elitism, sectarianism, formalism, and sexism, showing how none of these tendencies is in keeping with the essence and spirit of Buddhism. This is certainly good enough reason for its overwhelming emphasis on the need for genuine satori. And here if anywhere is the paradox of Zen: to attain satori it is necessary to get over these specious discriminations, or "attachments to form," as Keizan calls them; yet it is necessary to attain satori to finally get over them. This is why Dogen stated that practice and realization are nondual but that practice and realization under the auspices of the ego are delusion— thus strictly distinguishing between confusing and enlightening practice.

Similarly, *Transmission of Light* says: "Even if you sit until your seat breaks through, even if you persevere mindless of fatigue, even if you are a person of lofty deeds and pure behavior, if you haven't reached this realm of satori you still can't get out of the prison of the world. . . . Even if you are trained for many years and your thoughts are ended and your feelings are settled, your body like a dead tree and your heart like cold ashes, your mind never stirring in the face of events, even if you finally die sitting or standing and seem to have attained freedom in life and death, still if you haven't reached this realm it is all of no use in the house of the enlightened. . . . There is nothing to be delighted about in just being a Buddhist initiate in form—if you do not understand this matter, in the end you're no different from worldly people."

The whole format of *Transmission of Light*, ever at pains to help readers transcend superficial externals, is a guidebook to a universal enlightenment beyond cultural conditions. In India alone there were considerable changes in social and cultural conditions over the centuries between the arising of Buddhism and its transmission to China—and it is hard to imagine any two cultures as different as those of India and China. Even China and Japan, despite close cultural ties, are very different in terms of the ordinary mentality as conditioned by their respective societies. The languages of these three countries—representing Indo-European, Sinic, and Altaic families, radically different in structure and logic—are an illustration of the enormous disparity between the characteristic thought processes of these cultures.

Yet Zen insists that the fundamental human mind underlying all these circumstantially conditioned differences is one. The pervading thread of *Transmission of Light* is a grand illustration of how people can realize this unity in a manner more direct and profound than cross-cultural understanding as ordinarily conceived. Even if the form of the legends and tales in this particular text may be historically "soft," the transmission of Buddhism into such diverse Asian civilizations is the larger evidence of this simple "one mind" to which the quintessential Zen of this text is pointing.

Although it uses a quasi-historical format relating to the theoretical origins of Zen and the Soto school, *Transmission of Light* makes no reference to the lineage of masters in its story line as a symbol or proof of authority. Never does it use the idea of connection to the ancients for the purpose of enhancing the prestige of the author's school; rather, it uses the prestige of the ancients to evoke a sense of shame—one of the most powerful tools of Japanese psychology—in the followers of the school. There is in *Transmission of Light* none of the sectarianism and formalism later associated with certain sects of Soto Zen to the detriment of a general appreciation of the wider range of Soto teaching.

In eighteenth-century Japan there was considerable controversy over this issue in connection with the question of transmission and succession in Zen. One of the greatest masters of the age insisted that mind-to-mind communication in Zen was just that—requiring no institutional or sectarian affiliation and no personal relationship—in contrast to the originator of a school of formalists, among whose successors the "transmission of the teaching" was carried out through doctrine and elaborate ritual and depended on personal and institutional association.

Transmission of Light demonstrates how enlightenment and formal successorship do not necessarily take place in the same school or even in the same general lineage. One notorious example of this phenomenon is the patching of the last Chinese Soto lineage by a master of a completely different line. The direct Soto lineage died out in China when all the enlightened disciples of the last great master passed on before him, and the only person left in his school who knew all the teachings was denied successorship because of his competitiveness and desire to be ahead of others—common human weaknesses regarded as forms of mental illness in Zen. This patching operation is not only acknowledged in *Transmission of Light*, it is even emphasized to show that satori transcends sect. In a famous medieval Soto sectarian hagiography of the founder Dogen, on the other hand, the patching is vehemently denied on the alleged authority of a secret text that no one has ever seen. This particular contradiction is an excellent illustration of one difference between enlightened Soto Zen and sectarian Soto cultism.

The whole issue of Zen transmission and succession has a checkered history. In one sense, the very idea of transmission or succession may seem to suggest that there is actually something "passed on" from teacher to disciple; but this is denied in both scripture and classical Zen teaching, which says that the Zen experience is not passed on from one person to another as a form, doctrine, or hypnotic suggestion might be passed on. Communication of Zen is instead defined in terms of mutual recognition of awakened minds.

In his classic *Ten Guidelines for Zen Schools*, the great ninth-century Chinese master Fayan writes: "When the founder of Zen came from India to China, it was not because there was something to transmit; he just pointed directly to people's minds, so that they could see their essence and realize enlightenment—how could there be any sectarian styles to value?" In a similar vein, *Transmission of Light* says: "This truth is not received from Buddhas or Zen masters, it is not given to one's children, not inherited from one's parents." Zen proverb calls it "the subtlety that cannot be passed on even from father to son," and a line from a famous poem that also became proverbial says that "the one opening beyond is not transmitted by the sages."

The early Zen masters of China, all the way through the Tang dynasty (618–907), rarely even mention Zen successorship, much less make any claim to authority thereby. The few exceptions to this general rule involve special political and historical circumstances, and in any case they are not part of the broad mainstream of Zen tradition. During the Song dynasty (960–1278), with the dramatic increase of Confucian agitation against Buddhism and the establishment of a government-controlled public monastery system for Zen, there was more concern about Zen succession. Even then, however, a Zen master typically mentioned his succession only at the ceremony of opening of a teaching hall—and even then, while it may have satisfied Confucian demands for orthodoxy, in the context of uncontaminated Zen it was a symbol of humility and deference to ancient masters, not a mark of assertion and profession. As the Zen proverb says, "Good children don't use their parents' money."

By that time, of course, Zen had been effectively active in China for centuries, laying a basis for direct perception and common knowledge of both abstract and concrete signs of real Zen mastery that may or may not underlie individual claims to succession. In *Transmission of Light* it is noted, for example, that Rujing, the teacher of Dogen, never revealed his succession until the day he died. Yet he was appointed head teacher of several public monasteries, his mastery never in doubt, his tutelage sought even by Taoists.

After the Song dynasty, with the weakening of institutionalized Zen, there was increasing interest in lineage and transmission among some Zennists. Nevertheless, some of the most universally recognized Zen masters of the Ming dynasty (1368–1644) did not fit into any lineage at all. In Japan, on the other hand, where Zen was transmitted from Song dynasty China, in an era when institutionalized Zen had already been highly formalized and deeply corrupted, there was generally more intense interest in official succession than there had been in China. Adding to the historical circumstances of the founding of Zen in Japan was the fact that Japanese society is even more status-conscious than Chinese society, and the political and economic structure of religious organization in Japan was in general much more rigid than the ancient Zen of China.

In the history of Soto Zen there are a number of points where the matter of transmission is known to be confused, beginning with the very first generation after Dogen, where differing versions are given as to the number and identities of his successors. The middle ages show increasing complexity and unclarity, with multiple successions and a variety of ill-defined categories. This confusion was eventually replaced by statutory regulation imposed by government fiat in the late medieval and early modern periods. Therefore the ordinary licensing process known as "transmission of the teaching" in

xx   Transmission of Light

modern Soto Zen sects does not mean the same thing as the transmissions recorded in *Transmission of Light* and is not a direct continuation of the teachings of the masters in this lineage.

Indeed, it is a rather well publicized fact in Japan that satori has generally been lost in the dominant sect of Soto Zen for the last two or three hundred years. This sect became and remained institutionally strong, however, because of its persistent adherence to dogma, ritual, and conditioning, the very forces that hold every society on earth in spell. An attempt was made to rationalize this institutionalization by claiming that enlightenment is identical to the Soto training system, based on a fragmentary selection of bits and pieces from Dogen's writings. The other major surviving sect of Soto Zen, on the other hand, is descended from a master of the late seventeenth and early eighteenth centuries who vigorously upheld the teaching of satori and the formless reality of mutual recognition among enlightened minds. Because it was purer in its standards from a Zen standpoint, this school could not reproduce its effects mechanically and therefore is less well represented today, at least in numerical terms. Hence there is a general perception that Soto Zen deemphasizes or even denies satori. This, however, is not a complete picture at all.

There is at present no way for people in the modern West to verify the historical authenticity of any of the Zen lineages—in the sense of proving or disproving the understanding and teaching of each and every link in a lineage—to ascertain whether any deviation occurred along the way. There are, however, many universally accepted classical indications of what Zen is all about. The classics are more reliable than sectarian hagiographies as guides to determining authenticity in Zen, because unlike fragmentary historical records they can be proved in personal experience—and this can be done independently without social pressure to uphold any particular claim to authority. One of the proverbial guidelines for Zen study is: "First awaken on your own, then see someone else." As a handbook of method, *Transmission of Light* is a classic guide to "awakening on your own." As a collection of criteria, it is a way to "see someone else."

Transmission
of Light

I

Shakyamuni Buddha

Shakyamuni Buddha realized enlightenment on seeing the morning star. He said, "I and all beings on earth together attain enlightenment at the same time."

Shakyamuni left his palace one night when he was nineteen years old and shaved off his hair. After that he spent six years practicing ascetic exercises. Subsequently he sat on an indestructible seat, so immobile that there were cobwebs in his brows, a bird's nest on his head, and reeds growing up through his mat. Thus he sat for six years.

In his thirtieth year, on the eighth day of the twelfth month, he was suddenly enlightened when the morning star appeared. Then he spoke the foregoing words, his first lion roar.

After that he spent forty-nine years helping others by teaching, never staying in seclusion. With just one robe and one bowl, he lacked nothing. He taught at over three hundred and sixty assemblies, and then finally entrusted the treasury of the eye of truth to Kasyapa, and its transmission has continued to the present. Indeed, this is the root of the transmission and practice of the true teaching in India, China, and Japan.

The behavior of Shakyamuni Buddha during his lifetime is a model for the disciples he left behind. Even though he may have had the thirty-two special marks of greatness and the eighty kinds of refinements, he kept the form of an old mendicant, no different from anyone else.

Therefore, ever since he was in the world, through the three periods of his teaching—genuine, imitation, and derelict—those who have sought the way of his teaching have imitated the Buddha's form and manners, have used the endowment of the Buddha, and in all their doings have always considered the task of self-understanding foremost. Having been transmitted from Buddha to Buddha, from adept to adept, the true teaching has never been cut off. This story clearly points to this.

Even though what the Buddha pointed out and explained in the more than three hundred and sixty meetings over forty-nine years was not the same, the various stories, parables, metaphors, and explanations did not go beyond the principle illustrated in the story of his enlightenment.

That is to say, "I" is not Shakyamuni Buddha—even Shakyamuni Buddha comes from this "I." And it does not only give birth to Shakyamuni Buddha—"all beings on earth" also come from here. Just as when you lift up a net all the holes are raised, in the same way when Shakyamuni Buddha was enlightened so too were all beings on earth enlightened. And it was not only all beings on earth that were enlightened—all the Buddhas of past, present, and future also attained enlightenment.

While this is so, do not think of Shakyamuni Buddha as having become enlightened—do not see Shakyamuni Buddha outside of all beings on earth.

However immensely diverse the mountains, rivers, land, and all forms and appearances may be, all of them are in the eye of the Buddha. And you too are standing in the eye of the Buddha. And it is not simply that you are standing there—the eye has become you. Buddha's eye has become everyone's whole body, each standing tall.

Therefore this clear bright eye that spans all time should not be thought of as the people evidently here—you are Buddha's eye, Buddha is your whole body.

This being so, what do you call the principle of enlightenment? I ask you, is the Buddha enlightened with you? Are you enlightened with the Buddha? If you say you become enlightened with the Buddha or you say the Buddha becomes enlightened with you, this is not the Buddha's enlightenment at all. Therefore it should not be called the principle of enlightenment.

Even so, "I" and "together" are neither one nor two. Your skin, flesh, bones, and marrow are all "together," and the host inside the house is "I." It does not have skin, flesh, bones, or marrow, it does not have gross physical or mental elements. Ultimately speaking, "If you want to know the undying person in the hut, how could it be apart from this skin bag?" So you should not understand the beings on earth as distinct from yourself.

While the seasons come and go, and the mountains, rivers, and land change with the times, you should know that this is Buddha raising his eyebrows and blinking his eyes—so it is the "unique body revealed in myriad forms." It is "effacing myriad forms" and "not effacing myriad forms." The ancient master Fayan said, "What effacing or not effacing can you talk about?" And Dizang said, "What do you call myriad forms?"

So, studying from all angles, penetrating in all ways, you should clarify Buddha's enlightenment and understand your own enlightenment. I want you all to see this story closely and be able to explain it, letting the explanation flow from your own heart, not borrowing the words of another.

I also want to add a humble saying to this story:

One branch stands out on the old apricot tree;
Thorns come forth at the same time.

2

Kasyapa

When the Buddha raised a flower and blinked his eyes, Kasyapa broke out in a smile. The Buddha said, "I have the treasury of the eye of truth, the ineffable mind of nirvana. These I entrust to Kasyapa."

Kasyapa was born in a Brahmin family. In Sanskrit, Kasyapa means "Drinker of Light." When he was born, a golden light filled the room, then went into his mouth. Hence he was called Kasyapa, Drinker of Light. His complexion was golden, and he had thirty of the thirty-two major marks of greatness.

Kasyapa met the Buddha at a shrine known as the Shrine of Many Children. The Buddha said, "Welcome, mendicant," Kasyapa having already shaved his head and put on a patchwork vestment. Then the Buddha entrusted him with the treasury of the eye of truth. Kasyapa practiced austerities, and never wasted any time.

Only seeing the ugly emaciation of his body and the wretchedness of his clothing, everyone doubted Kasyapa. Because of this, every time the Buddha was going to give a talk in some place or other, he shared his seat with Kasyapa, who thenceforth was the senior member of the community.

Kasyapa was not only the senior member of Shakyamuni Buddha's community; he was the intrepid leader of the communities of all the Buddhas of the past. You should know that he was an ancient Buddha—do not just class him with the other disciples of Buddha.

Before an assembly of eighty thousand on Spiritual Mountain, the Buddha raised a flower and blinked his eyes. No one knew his meaning, all remained silent. Then Kasyapa alone broke into a smile. The Buddha said, "I have the treasury of the eye of truth, the ineffable mind of nirvana, and the formless teaching of complete illumination. I entrust it all to Kasyapa."

The so-called raising of the flower at that time has been transmitted purely through a succession of masters, not erroneously allowing outsiders to know about it. Therefore it is unknown to professors of doctrines and to many teachers of meditation. Obviously they do not know the reality.

Furthermore, this story, such as it is, is not a record of the assembly on Spiritual Mountain; these words were spoken in entrustment of the bequest at the Shrine of Many Children. The records that say it took place on Spiritual Mountain are wrong. When the teaching of enlightenment was bequeathed, there was this kind of "ceremony." Therefore if he were not a master bearing the seal of the enlightened mind, Kasyapa would not have known the time of that raising of the flower, and he would not have understood that raising of the flower.

Investigate carefully, see thoroughly—know that Kasyapa is Kasyapa, understand Shakyamuni Buddha as Shakyamuni Buddha, and simply transmit the Way of complete enlightenment in depth.

Leaving aside the raising of the flower for the moment, everyone should clearly understand the blinking of the eyes. You raise your eyebrows and blink your eyes in the ordinary course of things, and Buddha blinked his eyes when he raised the flower—these are not separate at all. Your talking and smiling, and Kasyapa's breaking into a smile, are not different at all.

But if you do not clearly understand the one who raised his eyebrows and blinked his eyes, then in India there is Shakyamuni Buddha, there is Kasyapa, and in your own mind there is skin, flesh, bones, and marrow. So many optical illusions, so much floating dust—you have never been free of them for countless eons, and you surely will be sunk in them for eons to come.

Once you come to know the inner self, you will find that Kasyapa can wriggle his toes in your shoes. Do you not realize that where

Shakyamuni raised his eyebrows and blinked his eyes, Shakyamuni immediately died away; and that where Kasyapa broke into a smile, Kasyapa immediately became enlightened? Is this not then one's own?

The treasury of the eye of truth is entrusted to oneself, and therefore you cannot call it Kasyapa or Shakyamuni. There has never been anything given to another, and there has never been anything received from anyone; this is called the truth.

Wanting to reveal Kasyapa, Shakyamuni held up a flower to show unchanging, and Kasyapa smiled to show longevity. In this way teacher and apprentice see each other and the lifeline flows through. Completely enlightened knowledge has nothing to do with thoughts. Kasyapa correctly cut through his conceptual faculty and went into Kukkutapada Mountain, awaiting the birth of the future Buddha Maitreya. Therefore Kasyapa even now has not become extinct.

If you study the Way sincerely and investigate it through in every detail, not only is Kasyapa not extinct but Shakyamuni too is eternal. Therefore since before you were born it has been pointed out directly and communicated simply, extending over all time, met with everywhere. Therefore you should not look to two thousand years in the past. If you just work on the Way with alacrity today, Kasyapa will be able to appear in the world today, without going into Kukkutapada Mountain.

Thus the flesh on Shakyamuni's body will still be warm and Kasyapa's smile will be renewed. If you can reach this realm, you will succeed to Kasyapa, and yet Kasyapa will be your heir. It has not only come from the seven Buddhas of antiquity to you; you can even be the root teacher of the seven Buddhas. Beginningless and endless, beyond the passage of time, the transmission of the treasury of the eye of truth will still be there.

Thus Shakyamuni Buddha also received the bequest of Kasyapa and is now in the heaven of satisfaction, the abode of imminent Buddhas, and you are also in the assembly on Spiritual Mountain, unchanging. Have you not heard the saying, "Always abiding on the Spiritual Mountain and other dwelling places, my land here will be safe and secure when the great fire burns, always filled with celestials and humans." This refers not only to the abode of the assembly on Spiritual Mountain—how could anywhere be left out? The true teaching of Buddha has spread without any lack.

Then this assembly here must be the assembly on Spiritual Mountain, while that assembly on Spiritual Mountain must be this assembly here. The Buddhas have only appeared and disappeared depending on your diligence or lack of it. Even today, if you work on the Way over and over, and pass through it in every detail, Shakyamuni Buddha immediately appears in the world. It is just because you do not understand yourselves that Shakyamuni passed away in olden times; since you are children of Buddha, how could you kill the Buddha? So get to work on the Way and meet your loving father.

Old Shakyamuni Buddha is with you all the time, whatever you are doing; he is conversing and exchanging greetings with you, never apart from you for a moment. If you never see him, you will be remiss, and even the hands of a thousand Buddhas will not reach you.

I have some humble words to point out this principle:

Know that in the remote recesses of the misty valley
There is another sacred pine that passes the winter cold.

3

Ananda

Ananda asked Kasyapa, "What did the Buddha hand on to you besides the golden-sleeved robe?"

Kasyapa said, "Ananda!"

Ananda said, "Yes?"

Kasyapa said, "Take down the banner pole in front of the gate."

Ananda was greatly enlightened.

Ananda was from the warrior caste, a cousin of Shakyamuni Buddha. "Ananda" means happiness or joy; he was born the night of the Buddha's enlightenment, and he was so extraordinarily handsome that everyone was happy to see him—hence his name.

Ananda was foremost in learning, intellectually brilliant and broad in understanding. He was the Buddha's attendant for twenty years, propagated all of the Buddha's teachings, and studied all of the Buddha's manners. When the Buddha entrusted the treasury of the eye of truth to Kasyapa, he also instructed Ananda to help communicate the teaching. So Ananda accompanied Kasyapa for twenty more years and became thoroughly familiar with the entire treasury of the eye of truth.

This should document the fact that the way of Zen is not in the same class as other schools. Ananda was already foremost in learning, having studied widely and gained a broad understanding, with the Buddha himself giving him approval many times—yet he did not hold the transmission of truth or attain illumination of the ground of mind.

When Kasyapa was going to compile the teachings left by the Buddha, Ananda was not permitted to attend because he had not yet attained realization. Then Ananda meditated carefully and soon attained sainthood. When he went to go into the room where the teachings were being compiled, Kasyapa told him that if he had attained realization he should enter by a show of supernormal powers. So Ananda appeared in a tiny body and went in through the keyhole. Thus he was finally able to enter.

The disciples all said, "Ananda was the Buddha's attendant, so he has heard a lot and studied widely. It was like a cup of water poured into another cup, without spilling anything. Let us ask Ananda to recite the teachings for us."

So Kasyapa said to Ananda, "Everyone is looking to you to recite the sayings of the Buddha."

Then Ananda, who had kept the bequest of the Buddha within him, and had now also received this request of Kasyapa, began to recite all the teachings of the Buddha's lifetime.

Kasyapa said to the disciples, "Is this any different from what the Buddha taught?"

The disciples said, "It is no different."

The disciples in attendance were all great saints with the six superknowledges, including the knowledge of past lives, clairvoyance, and knowledge of the end of contamination. They did not forget anything they had heard. With one voice they said, "Is this the Buddha's second coming, or is this Ananda talking?" They said in praise, "The waters of the ocean of the Buddha's teaching have flowed into Ananda."

The teachings of the Buddha that have come down through the present are those spoken by Ananda. So we know for certain this Way does not depend on great learning or on the attainment of realization; this should be proof. Ananda still followed Kasyapa for twenty years, and he was first greatly enlightened at the time of the event cited in the beginning.

Since he was born the night of the Buddha's enlightenment,

Ananda did not hear such discourses as the Flower Ornament Scripture, but he attained the concentration of awareness of Buddha and could recite what he had not heard. That he nevertheless had not entered the Way of Zen is just the same as our failure to enter.

In the distant past, Ananda had awakened the aspiration for complete perfect enlightenment in the presence of the Buddha called King of Emptiness, at the same time as did the present Buddha Shakyamuni. Ananda was fond of intellectual learning, and that is why he had not yet truly realized enlightenment. Shakyamuni, on the other hand, cultivated energy, whereby he attained true enlightenment. Surely much academic learning is a hindrance on the Way—here is proof of that. This is why the Flower Ornament Scripture says, "Much learning without practical application is like a poor man counting another's treasures without half a cent of his own."

If you want to find out what this Way really is, do not be fond of academic learning, just be energetic in progressive practice.

Yet I daresay that there must be something besides the handing on of the robe. Thus Ananda once said to Kasyapa, "The Buddha bequeathed the golden-sleeved robe to you; what else did he transmit?" Kasyapa, realizing the time was ripe, called "Ananda!" When Ananda responded, Kasyapa said, "Take down the banner pole in front of the gate." Ananda was greatly enlightened as he heard this; the Buddha's robe spontaneously entered the top of Ananda's head.

That golden-sleeved robe was the vestment transmitted and kept by the seven Buddhas of antiquity. There are three explanations of that robe. One is that the Buddha brought it with him from the womb, another is that it was given by a being of the heaven of pure abodes, and the third is that it was presented by a hunter.

There are several other vestments of the Buddha. The vestment transmitted from Bodhidharma through the first six Zen founders in China was made of blue-black muslin. When it came to China, a blue-green lining was put in. It is now kept in the shrine of the sixth founder and is considered a national treasure. This is the one mentioned in the Treatise on Transcendent Wisdom, where it says, "The Buddha put on a coarse monk's garment."

The golden sleeves were golden felt. A scripture says that the Buddha's aunt made a vestment of golden felt by herself and gave it to the Buddha.

These are only one or two of many vestments. As for the miracles associated with them, they are found in many scriptural passages containing situational teachings.

In ancient times, when the Buddhist master Vashashita was challenged by an evil king, the Buddha's robe emanated light of five colors while in a fire, and when the fire was extinguished the vestment was unharmed. The king then believed it was the Buddha's vestment. It is that which will be transmitted to Maitreya.

The treasury of the eye of truth was not transmitted to two people; only one person, Kasyapa, received the Buddha's bequest. Moreover, Ananda attended Kasyapa for twenty years and held the transmission of the teaching. Thus the Zen school should be known to be a special transmission outside of doctrine, but recently it has thoughtlessly come to be considered the same as doctrinal schools.

If they were one and the same, since Ananda was a saint with the six superknowledges, he would have received the Buddha's bequest and would have been the Buddha's successor. Was there anyone who understood the teachings of the scriptures better than Ananda? If there were anyone surpassing Ananda in this regard, then it could be admitted that the idea of the scriptures is one and the same as the meaning of Zen. If you say they are just one, why would Ananda take the trouble to attend Kasyapa for twenty years and become illumined at the command "Take down the banner pole"? Know that the idea of the scriptures is not to be considered the Way of Zen.

It is not that Buddha was not a Buddha, but even if Ananda was his attendant, how could he transmit to him the mind seal as long as he had not penetrated the enlightened mind? You should realize that this does not depend on having a lot of academic learning. Even if you can memorize the sacred teachings in books perfectly by means of your intelligence, if you do not penetrate the heart it is like uselessly counting another's treasures. It is not that the heart is not in the scriptural teachings, but that Ananda had not yet penetrated it. The literalist interpreters in the Far East fail to penetrate the heart of the scriptures.

You should also realize that the way of enlightenment is not easy. When Ananda, who was versed in the sacred teachings of the Buddha's whole lifetime, propagated them as the disciple of Buddha, who would not go along? Nevertheless you should know he attended Kasyapa and again propagated the teachings after his great enlightenment. It was like fire joining fire.

If you want to reach the true path clearly, you should give up your idea of self, your old feelings of conceit and self-importance, and return to the pristine inspired mind to comprehend enlightened knowledge.

As for the incident in Ananda's enlightenment story, Ananda thought that Kasyapa had received the golden-sleeved vestment and was a disciple of Buddha, and that there was nothing special other than that. Nevertheless, after following Kasyapa and attending him closely, he thought Kasyapa had realized something more. Kasyapa then knew that the time was right, and called to Ananda. Like a valley spirit echoing in response to a call, Ananda replied immediately, like a spark issuing from a flint. Although Kasyapa called "Ananda," he was not calling Ananda, and Ananda did not echo in reply.

As for "Take down the banner pole in front of the gate," it refers to a custom of India. When the Buddhists and followers of other religions and philosophies would set to debate, both sides would put up a banner; when one side was defeated, their banner would be torn down. The present incident seems to suggest that Kasyapa and Ananda had set up their banners next to each other; since now Ananda was appearing in the world, Kasyapa should fold up his banner—one appearing, one disappearing.

But this is not what the story means. If Kasyapa and Ananda are both banner poles, the principle is not evident. Once a banner pole is taken down, another banner pole should appear. When Kasyapa instructed Ananda to take down the banner pole in front of the gate, Ananda was greatly enlightened because he realized the communion of the paths of teacher and apprentice.

After his enlightenment, Ananda took down even Kasyapa, and mountains and rivers all crumbled away. Hence the Buddha's robe naturally entered the crown of Ananda's head.

But do not use this story to remain in the state of "standing like a mile-high wall in the mass of naked flesh." Do not linger in purity. You should go on to realize that there is a valley spirit. Buddhas appeared in the world one after another; the Zen masters pointed it out generation after generation. It was only this matter; the mind-to-mind communication was ultimately unknown to others.

Even if the obvious masses of naked flesh, Kasyapa and Ananda, are one or two faces of the appearance in the world of "That One," do not consider Kasyapa and Ananda as "That One." Now each of you stands like a wall a mile high, you are myriad transformations of "That One." If you know "That One," you will be buried at once. If so, one should not look for "taking down the banner pole" outside of oneself.

Again I want to add some words:

The vines withered, the trees fallen,
The mountains crumble away—
The valley stream swells in a torrent,
Sparks fly from stone.

4

Shanavasa

Shanavasa asked Ananda, "What is the fundamental uncreated essence of all things?"

Ananda pointed to the corner of Shanavasa's vest.

Shanavasa asked, "What is the basic essence of the enlightenment of the Buddhas?"

Ananda grabbed the corner of Shanavasa's vest and tugged on it.

Shanavasa was then enlightened.

In Sanskrit, Shanavasa means "Natural Clothing." When Shanavasa was born, he came wearing clothing. In summer it became cool clothing, in winter it became warm clothing. When he was inspired to leave society, his ordinary clothing spontaneously turned into a mendicant's vestment.

Shanavasa did not just happen to be born this way in his present lifetime; when he was a merchant in a past life, he gave a hundred Buddhas a thousand feet of felt, and ever since then he wore natural clothing in every life. Usually people refer to the interval between giving up present existence and before reaching future existence by the term "intermediate existence." During that time they wear no clothing.

"Shanavasa" is also the name of an Indian plant called "Nine Branch Beauty." When a saint is born, this plant grows on clear ground. When Shanavasa was born this plant grew, and that is why he was named Shanavasa.

He was in the womb for six years before birth. In the past the Buddha had pointed to a forest and said, "In this wood a mendicant named Shanavasa will turn the wheel of the sublime teaching a hundred years after my death." As it turned out, Shanavasa was born there a century later, eventually received the bequest of Ananda, and stayed in this forest. Turning the wheel of the teaching, he overcame a fire dragon; the fire dragon submitted to him and offered him this forest. This was indeed in accord with the prediction of the Buddha.

Originally, however, Shanavasa was a sorcerer from the Himalaya mountains. After becoming a disciple of Ananda, he asked, "What is the fundamental uncreated essence of all things?" This is in fact something that no one but Shanavasa had ever asked. The fundamental uncreated essence of all things is in everyone, yet they do not know they have it, nor do they ask.

Why is it called the uncreated essence? Though all things are born from it, this essence has no producer, so it is called the uncreated essence. Therefore everything is fundamentally uncreated—mountains are not mountains, rivers are not rivers. This is why Ananda pointed to the corner of Shanavasa's vest.

This vest is called *kashaya* in Sanskrit; this means indefinite color, and it means unborn color. Actually it is not to be seen in terms of color. Yet in one sense, the subjective and objective experiences of all beings, from Buddhas to insects, are all colored. But this is not the color perceived by the ordinary senses, so there is no world to transcend, no enlightenment to realize.

Even though he understood this, Shanavasa went on to ask, "What is the fundamental essence of enlightenment of the Buddhas?" Although there has never been any mistake in this, unless you find out that you have it, you will be uselessly hindered by your eyes. This is why Shanavasa asked this question: to clarify the source of all Buddhas.

Responding to the call, Ananda deliberately tugged on Shanavasa's vest to let him know that the Buddhas come out in response to the search for them. Shanavasa was thereupon greatly enlightened.

Although that which never has been off is like this, you cannot ever realize that it is your own wisdom-mother of all Buddhas unless you come across it once.

This is why the Buddhas have appeared in the world one after another, and why the Zen masters have taught generation after generation. Although there has never been anything to give to anyone or anything to receive from anyone, it is necessary to experience this as intimately as feeling the nose on your own face.

Zen study demands that you investigate and awaken on your own. After awakening, you should meet others who are enlightened. If you do not meet anyone enlightened, you will just become obsessive and cannot be called a Zen seeker.

It should be clear from this story of Shanavasa that you should not waste your life. You should not just be a spontaneous naturalist, and you should not prefer your idea of yourself or your former views.

You may think that Buddhist Zen is just for special people and that you are not fit for it, but such ideas are the worst kind of folly. Who among the ancients was not a mortal? Whose personality was not influenced by social and material values? Once they studied Zen, however, they penetrated all the way through.

There may have been differences in periods of true, imitative, and decadent Buddhism in India, China, and Japan, yet there have been plenty of saints and sages who realized the fruits of Buddhism. Since you have the same faculties as the ancients, so wherever you are you are still human beings. Your physical and mental elements are no different from those of Kasyapa and Ananda, so why should you be different from the ancients with respect to enlightenment?

It is only by failure to find out the truth and master the Way that you lose the human body in vain, without ever realizing what you have in yourself.

Ananda took Kasyapa as his teacher because he learned that he should not waste his life, and for this reason he also accepted Shanavasa as a disciple. Thus the Way was transmitted from teacher to apprentice. The treasury of the eye of truth and the ineffable mind of nirvana communicated in this way are no different from when the Buddha was in the world.

Therefore do not regret that you were not born in the land of the Buddha's birthplace, and do not lament that you have not met the Buddha living in the world. In the past you planted seeds of virtue and formed affinity with wisdom; it is because of this that you have gathered here in this congregation.

This is indeed like standing shoulder to shoulder with Kasyapa, sitting knee to knee with Ananda. So while we may be host and guests for a day, you will be Buddhas and Zen masters all of your lives.

Do not get stuck in objects of sense, do not pass the nights and days in vain. Work on the Way carefully, reach the ultimate point to which the ancients penetrated, and receive the seal of enlightenment and directions for the future in the present day.

I have another verse to clarify the present story:

The sourceless river on a mountain miles high—
Piercing rocks, sweeping clouds, it surges forth;
Scattering clouds, sending flowers flying in profusion,
The length of white silk is absolutely free of dust.

5

Upagupta

Upagupta attended Shanavasa for three years, then finally shaved his head and became a mendicant. Shanavasa asked him, "Are you leaving home physically or mentally?"

Upagupta said, "Actually I am leaving home physically."

Shanavasa said, "What has the sublime truth of the Buddhas to do with body or mind?"

On hearing this, Upagupta was enlightened.

Upagupta was from the peasant caste. He called on Shanavasa when he was fifteen years old, became a mendicant when he was seventeen, and realized enlightenment when he was twenty-two.

In his teaching travels, Upagupta came to Mathura, where those who attained salvation were most numerous. Because of this, the palace of demons quaked and the devil was distressed and dismayed.

Whenever anyone attained realization, Upagupta would cast a talisman four fingers in breadth into a cave. The cave was eighteen cubits by twelve cubits, and it was filled with talismans—that is how many people attained enlightenment.

When Upagupta died, he was cremated with the talismans representing those whom he had enlightened. As many people were liberated by him as had been liberated in the time of the Buddha, so Upagupta was called a buddha without special marks.

In anger the devil watched for when Upagupta would enter meditation, and then used all his devilish power to try to destroy the truth.

Upagupta went into concentration trance and saw what was going on. The devil, perceiving this, came and put a garland on Upagupta's neck. Upagupta, wishing to subdue the devil, rose from meditation, transformed a human corpse, a dead dog, and a dead snake into a flower garland, and spoke gently to the devil, saying, "You gave me a fine necklace, and now I have a flower garland to offer you in return."

The devil happily extended his neck to receive it, whereupon the garland turned back into the three stinking corpses, infested and rotting. The devil was disgusted and greatly upset, but he could not get rid of the garland even with all his magical powers. He ascended to the six heavens of desire and told the gods there about this, and also went to the heaven of Brahma seeking to be liberated. They all told him that it was an occult manifestation of the powers of an enlightened Buddhist, and they could do nothing about it. When the devil asked them what he should do, the gods told him that he could get rid of the necklace of corpses if he became Upagupta's disciple. Then they sent him back with a verse:

> If you fall on the ground, you must rise from the ground;
> It is impossible to stand apart from the ground.
> You must seek liberation from a Buddhist of enlightened
>   powers.

So the devil descended from the heavens, prostrated himself at Upagupta's feet, and repented. Upagupta said, "Will you create any more trouble for the true teaching of Buddha?" The devil promised to dedicate himself to the Way of Buddha and to stop evil forever. Upagupta said, "Then you should declare refuge in the Three Treasures, the Buddha, the Teaching, and the Community." The devil repeated the refuge-taking formula thrice, whereupon the garland of corpses fell off. In this way did Upagupta demonstrate the powerful effect of Buddhism, just as when the Buddha was alive in the world.

When Upagupta had his head shaved at the age of seventeen, Shanavasa asked him, "Are you leaving home in body or in mind?" In Buddhism there are basically two kinds of home-leaving—that of body and that of mind.

Those who leave home physically give up social and personal sentiments, leave their native place, shave off their hair and dress in black, and do not have any servants, becoming mendicants. They work on the Way twenty-four hours a day, so they waste no time and have no extraneous desires. Therefore they are not happy to be alive and do not fear to die. Their minds are like the pure clarity of the autumn moon, their eyes are like the flawlessness of a bright mirror. They do not seek mind or look for essence; they do not even practice the holy truths, much less have any worldly attachments. In this way they do not remain in the state of ordinary mortals, nor are they confined to the state of sages and saints—they are mindless wayfarers. These are people who leave home physically.

Those who leave home mentally do not shave off their hair or wear special clothing. Though they live at home and are in the midst of the troubles of the world, they are like lotuses unsoiled by mud, like jewels unaffected by dust. Even though they may have spouses and children according to circumstances, they are not attached to them. Like the moon in the sky, like a pearl rolling in a bowl, they see the one who is free in the midst of a bustling city, they understand beyond time while in the world, they know that "even cutting off passions is a disease," and realize that "aiming for true thusness is also wrong." To them, nirvana and samsara are both illusions; they are concerned with neither enlightenment nor affliction. These are people who leave home mentally.

Therefore Shanavasa asked Upagupta, "Are you leaving home physically or mentally?" He asked this question because otherwise a home-leaver is not a home-leaver.

Upagupta answered, "Actually I am leaving home physically." Here he was not thinking of mind, talking about essence, or discussing mystery. He only knew that the elemental body leaves home. It comes without movement, so he understood it to be spiritual power; it is gotten without seeking, so he understood it to be ungraspable. Therefore he said he was actually leaving home physically.

But the subtle truth of the Buddhas should not be seen or understood in this way, so Shanavasa explained to him that the Buddhas actually do not leave home physically or mentally—they are not to be seen in terms of matter or of psychological and physical elements, and cannot be witnessed in terms of noumenon or mystery.

Therefore the Buddhas are free from both the sacred and the profane; they have shed both mind and body alike. They are like space, without outside or inside, like the water of the ocean. No matter how numerous and diverse their many subtle principles and innumerable teachings, all of them explain only this thing.

Therefore "The Sole Honored One" should not be called Buddha, nor should we refer to it as "not coming or going." Who says "before your parents were born" or "before the empty eon"?

When you get here, you transcend birth and nonbirth, you are liberated from mind and nonmind. It is like water conforming to the vessel, like things resting on space. Though you grasp, your hand is not full; though you search, you cannot find a trace. This is the subtle truth of the Buddhas.

At this point Upagupta no longer existed, nor did Shanavasa; therefore they did not employ motion or stillness, going or coming. Even if there were affirmation and negation, other and self, it was like sound underwater, like the boundlessness of space.

Furthermore, if you do not experience this once, even millions of teachings and their infinite subtle principles will all uselessly become flows of habitual consciousness.

When this was pointed out to him, Upagupta was suddenly enlightened. It was like thunder in a clear sky, like a raging fire springing up on the ground. Once the swift thunder pealed, not only were Upagupta's ears cut off, he immediately lost his root of life. The blazing fire suddenly burning, the teachings of the Buddhas and the heads of the Zen masters all became ashes.

These ashes have appeared under the name Upagupta, hard as stone, black as lacquer. How many people's original forms were lost, their whole bodies pulverized—he cast talismans counting voidness, finally burning emptiness and leaving empty traces.

Today, as his descendant, I want to look for tracks beyond the clouds and stick worlds up in the clear sky:

The house broken up, the people gone, neither inside nor out,
Where have body and mind ever hidden their forms?

6

Dhrtaka

Dhrtaka said, "One who renounces the world has no personal self, no personal possessions, so is mentally neither aroused nor oblivious. This is the eternal Way. The Buddhas too are eternal. The mind has no shape or form, and its essence is also thus."

Upagupta said, "You should completely awaken and attain this in your own mind."

Dhrtaka was thereupon greatly enlightened.

When Dhrtaka was born, his father dreamed a golden sun came out from the house and illumined heaven and earth. In the foreground was a huge mountain magnificently adorned with jewels; at the summit of the mountain welled forth a spring, flowing in four directions.

When Dhrtaka first met Upagupta, he told him about this dream. Upagupta interpreted it for him: "The great mountain is me; the welling spring means the pouring forth of your wisdom and truth without end. The sun emerging from the house is a sign of your present entry into the Way. The illumination of heaven and earth is transcendence through wisdom."

Hearing Upagupta's explanation, Dhrtaka chanted a verse:

The magnificent mountain of jewels
Always produces the spring of wisdom;

It turns into the flavor of real truth
Liberating those with affinity.

Upagupta also chanted a verse:

My teaching is bequeathed to you;
You should show great wisdom,
As the sun emerging from the house
Illumines heaven and earth.

Henceforth Dhrtaka became a disciple of Upagupta and eventually sought to renounce the world to become a mendicant. Upagupta asked him, "You are intent on renouncing the world. Do you renounce the world in body or mind?"

Dhrtaka said, "I came seeking to renounce the world, not for the sake of body or mind."

Upagupta said, "Since it is not for body or mind, then who renounces the world?"

Dhrtaka said, "One who renounces the world has no personal self . . ." and so on, and finally he was greatly enlightened.

Actually, one who renounces the world shows the self that has no personal self; therefore it cannot be understood in terms of body or mind. This selfless self is the eternal Way; it cannot be fathomed in terms of birth and death. Therefore it is not the Buddhas, and it is not living beings—how could it be material or psychological elements, realms of desire, form, or formlessness, or sundry states of existence?

Thus the mind has no shape or form; even though it be seeing and hearing, discerning and knowing, ultimately it does not come or go, it is not moving or still.

One who sees in this way—that is, one who knows the mind—still must be said to understand on the basis of learning. For this reason, even though Dhrtaka understood in this way, Upagupta rapped him by saying, "You should awaken completely and realize this in your own mind."

It is like putting the imperial seal on an article of merchandise: when the imperial seal is on it, people know it is not poison, it is not suspicious, and it is not government property; therefore people use it. The merging of the paths of teacher and apprentice is like this: even if one understands all principles and comprehends all paths, one must still become greatly enlightened before really attaining.

If you are not greatly enlightened once, you will vainly become mere intellectuals and never arrive at the ground of mind. Because of this you are not yet rid of views of Buddha and Dharma, so when will you ever get out of the bondage of self and others?

Thus even if you can remember all the sermons spoken by the Buddha over his forty-nine years of teaching, and do not misunderstand a single doctrine of the three and five vehicles of liberation, if you do not greatly awaken once, you cannot be acknowledged as a true Zen adept. So even if you can expound a thousand scriptures and ten thousand treatises, cause the Buddhas to shed their light, cause the earth to tremble and the sky to shower flowers, this is just the understanding of a professor, not that of a real Zen adept.

So you should not understand in terms of "the world is only mind," and you should not understand in terms of "all things are characteristics of reality." You should not understand in terms of all existence being the essence of buddhahood, nor should you understand in terms of ultimate empty silence.

"The character of reality" is still involved in classification; "all is empty" is the same as decadent nihilism. "All existence" resembles spirit; "only mind" is still not free from conscious cognition. Therefore when those who would seek this matter seek it among the thousands of scriptures and myriads of treatises, unfortunately they are running away from their own progenitor.

So when you open up your own treasury in each case to bring forth the great treasure of the scriptures, you will naturally be able to have the holy teaching as your own. If you do not attain realization in this way, the Buddhas and Zen masters are all your enemies. That is why it is said, "What demon caused you to become a mendicant, what demon made you go traveling? Even if you can say, you will die on the hook; and if you cannot say, you will also die on the hook."

Thus it is said that the renunciation of the world is not for the sake of mind or body. But even though Dhrtaka had understood in this way, he was still not a true adept; he had to have it pointed out to him again before he was greatly enlightened and actually realized it.

So you should work on the Way carefully and continuously: without being literalists, and without interpreting spirituality subjectively, smash the universe completely. Without any obstruction even as you go back and forth between before and after, without any disparity even as you go in and out above and below, digging out a cave in space, rousing waves on level ground, see the face of Buddha, perceive enlightenment clarifying the mind, experience the unity of being and spin the pearl of perfect light—when you know there is something in the inner sanctum of Buddhas and Zen masters, then you will finally attain this.

I want to add a saying to this story:

When you attain the marrow, know the attainment is clear;
An adept still has an incommunicable subtlety.

7

Micchaka

Dhrtaka said to Micchaka, "To practice sorcery, thus learning something minor, is like being dragged by a rope. You should know for yourself that if you give up the little stream and immediately return to the great ocean, you will realize the uncreated."

On hearing this, Micchaka realized enlightenment.

Micchaka, who was from central India, was the leader of eight thousand sorcerers. One day he brought his followers to pay respects to the Buddhist master Dhrtaka and said to him, "In the past we both lived in the heaven of purity; I met the sorcerer Asita and learned the methods of sorcery, while you met a fully empowered Buddhist and practiced meditation. Thenceforth our lots differed and we have gone our separate ways, for six eons now."

Dhrtaka said, "Having spent eons apart, what a lesson this is indeed! Now you should give up the false and return to the true, thereby to enter the vehicle of enlightenment."

Micchaka said, "Long ago the sorcerer Asita predicted that after six eons I would meet a fellow student and realize the state of non-contamination. Is not our present meeting due to our past relation? Please be so kind and compassionate as to liberate me."

Dhrtaka then had Micchaka renounce worldliness and accept the Buddhist precepts. At first the other sorcerers were too conceited to follow suit, but then Dhrtaka showed great miraculous powers that inspired them all to seek enlightenment. So they all became mendicants at once.

When the eight thousand sorcerers therefore became eight thousand mendicants and wanted to follow him into homelessness, Dhrtaka said, "The Buddha said that to practice sorcery, studying what is minor, is like being dragged by a rope." Finally, after listening to Dhrtaka, Micchaka attained enlightenment.

Even if by studying sorcery you manage to prolong your life and attain supernormal powers, you can only comprehend eighty thousand eons past and future—you cannot see before or after that. Even though you cultivate the state in which there is neither perception nor nonperception and enter mindless thoughtless trance, unfortunately you will be born in the heaven beyond thought, become a long-lived celestial being, and still have the flowing stream of habitual consciousness even though you are rid of the material body. You cannot find the Buddha, cannot reach the Way. When the results of that active consciousness are exhausted, you will then fall into uninterrupted hell. That is why this is like being bound and dragged by a rope, so there is no chance of liberation.

Although students of individual Buddhist liberation realize four stages of attainment or individual enlightenment, this is still cultivation of body and mind, practice of the Way in terms of delusion and enlightenment. Because of this, saints of the first stage go through eighty thousand eons before they become freshly inspired universalists, saints of the second stage go through sixty thousand eons before they become freshly inspired universalists, and saints of the third stage go through forty thousand eons before they become freshly inspired universalists. Individually enlightened saints only enter the path of universal enlightenment after ten thousand eons. Although good causes eventually pay off, routine activity is regrettably not ended by this kind of practice. This too is like being dragged by a rope; these are not fundamentally liberated people.

Actually, even though you break up compulsions of views and thoughts with their infinite delusions, so that there is not a particle of material sense to control, not the slightest confusion, this is merely contrived effort and is not the undefiled realization of buddhahood.

Therefore all work on the Way that involves returning to the source and going back to the fountainhead, and which looks forward to enlightenment as a rule, is all of this category.

So do not even seek nothingness, for you may become the same as nihilists. You should not remain in the "eon of emptiness, before the primordial Buddha," for this too is to be like a corpse from which the spirit has not yet departed. Do not wish to stop illusions in order to arrive at reality, for this is the same as the saints who cut off ignorance to realize the middle way. This is producing clouds where there are no clouds, producing flaws where there are no flaws—you will become a destitute vagrant in a foreign country, an impoverished traveler drunk with ignorance.

Think about it. Since you are someone, you speak of before birth and after death; but what further past, present, or future could you think of? Always, without a moment's error, from birth to death it is just thus—but unless you encounter it once, you will vainly be confused by material senses, you will not know your own self. This is estrangement from what is right before your eyes.

Because of this you do not know where body and mind come from, you do not understand where myriad things come from. For no reason you want to eliminate something and seek something else. Thus you cause the Buddhas to bother with appearing in the world, you cause the Zen masters to bother with giving instructions. But even though they lend a hand in giving out instructions this way, you are still deluded by your own knowledge and views, you say that you don't know or don't understand. Yet you are not really ignorant; you are not actually boxed in—you are vainly discriminating views of right and wrong within your thoughts and judgments.

Do you not realize that you respond when called and you get where you are going by following directions? This does not come from deliberate thought or conscious knowledge—it is the host within you. That host has no face or physical features, yet it always moves without stopping. From this the mind comes into being. This is called the body. Once this body appears, various elements combine to form your individual body. It is just like a jewel having luster, like a sound bringing along an echo.

Thus there is never any lack or excess in birth and death. In such birth and death, though birth takes place, there is no beginning of birth, and though death takes place, there is no trace of death. It is like waves arising in the ocean, without any tracks, like the waves never dying out—though they go on and on, they never go anywhere else; it is only as a condition of the ocean that great and small waves arise endlessly.

Your mind is also like this. It moves ceaselessly, and so it appears as skin, flesh, bones, and marrow; it functions as matter, sensation, perception, activity, and consciousness. It also appears as peach blossoms and green bamboo, it realizes enlightenment as attainment of the Way and illumination of the mind, it works as speech and action. Though divided, it is not different; though manifesting and manifested, it does not remain in physical form. It is like a phantom exercising magical arts, it is like dreaming producing all sorts of images. Though myriad reflections in a mirror change in innumerable ways, it is just the same mirror. If you do not realize this, but vainly cultivate sorcery, studying a minor affair, there is no hope of liberation.

No one binds you—how can there be any further liberation? Delusion and enlightenment have never existed; bondage and liberation are irrelevant from the first. Is this not the uncreated? Is this not the ocean? Where are there any small streams?

Lands as many as atoms, as many as atomic particles, are all the ocean of the universe. Valley streams, rushing rapids, swirling rivers—all are movements of the ocean. So there are no small streams to abandon, there is no great ocean to grasp. This being so, all divisions gone of themselves, Micchaka's former views underwent a revolution; he gave up sorcery and abandoned worldliness. This was the activation of a preexisting affinity.

Furthermore, if you study and investigate continuously in this way, you will realize immediate communication by mind and by worlds. Truly this is a close friend meeting a close friend, it is oneself understanding oneself. All float and swim together in the ocean of nature, with never a gap. When you realize this, preexisting affinities must become evident.

The great master Mazu said, "Everyone has always been absorbed in the nature of reality, forever in absorption in the nature of reality, wearing clothing, eating food, speaking and conversing. All senses and capacities in action are none other than the nature of reality."

Hearing this, you should not take it to mean that there are beings within the nature of reality. To say "the nature of reality" and "beings" is like saying "water" and "waves." So in terms of words we may speak of water and waves, but is there really any difference?

Again I have a humble saying to explain this story:

> Though there be the purity of the autumn waters
> Extending to the horizon,
> How does that compare with the haziness
> Of a spring night's moon?
> Most people want clear purity,
> But though you sweep and sweep,
> The mind is not yet emptied.

8

Vasumitra

Vasumitra placed a wine vessel in front of Micchaka, bowed, and stood there. Micchaka asked him, "Is this my vessel or yours?" As Vasumitra thought it over, Micchaka said, "If you consider it my vessel, yet it is your inherent nature. Then again, if it is your vessel, you should receive my teaching."

Hearing this, Vasumitra understood the uncreated fundamental nature.

Vasumitra was from northern India, of the Bharadhvaja clan. He always wore clean clothing. He used to wander around the villages carrying a wine vessel, whistling and singing. People thought he was crazy. He did not reveal his clan name.

In the course of his teaching travels, the Buddhist master Micchaka came to northern India. As he looked over a wall, he saw auspicious golden clouds rising, and he said to his followers, "This is the aura of a man of the Way. There must be a great man here, one who is to be my spiritual successor."

Before Micchaka had finished speaking, Vasumitra showed up and asked him, "Do you know what is in my hand?"

Micchaka said, "It is an impure vessel, inappropriate for the pure."

Vasumitra then placed the vessel in front of Micchaka, and finally realized the uncreated fundamental nature. Then the wine vessel suddenly disappeared.

Micchaka then said, "Tell me your name, and I will tell you the past basis of your enlightenment."

Vasumitra replied, "For innumerable eons, even until my birth in this land, my clan has been Bharadhvaja, my name is Vasumitra."

Then Micchaka told him, "My teacher Dhrtaka told me that long ago when the Buddha was traveling in northern India he told Ananda, 'Three hundred years after my death there will be a saint in this country. He will be of the Bharadhvaja clan, his name will be Vasumitra, and he will be the seventh patriarch of Dhyana.' The Buddha predicted your career; you should leave the mundane."

Hearing this, Vasumitra said, "As I think back to the distant past, I remember that I was once a patron of religion and gave a jeweled chair to a Buddha. That Buddha predicted that I would succeed to sainthood in the religion of Shakyamuni Buddha."

Before he had met Micchaka, Vasumitra carried a wine vessel all the time, never letting go of it. Actually this is a representation. He used this vessel morning and night, employing it without inhibition. Really this represents his being a vessel of the teaching.

This is why he started his study by asking, "Do you know what I have in my hand?"

Even if you understand that "mind is the Way" and that "the body is Buddha," this is still a defiled vessel, and being a defiled vessel is inappropriate for the pure. You may understand that "it encompasses all time" and you may know that "it is forever complete," but all this is a defiled vessel. What past or present are you talking about? What beginning or end are you talking about? Views like this are inappropriate for the pure.

Realizing the impeccability of Micchaka's reasoning, Vasumitra then put aside the wine vessel. This represents his becoming a disciple of Micchaka, the enlightened Buddhist master.

This is why Micchaka asked, "Do you consider this my vessel or your vessel?" There was no question of past or present; it was beyond views of coming and going. At this point, do you think it is I, or do you think it is you?

As Vasumitra was thinking that it is neither "I" nor "you," Micchaka said to him, "If you consider it my vessel, yet it is your inherent nature." So it wasn't Micchaka's vessel. "Then again, if it is your vessel, you should receive my teaching." Therefore it wasn't Vasumitra's vessel either. It is not "my" vessel or "your" vessel, so the vessel itself is not even a vessel. This is why the vessel thereupon disappeared.

This whole story is not something that people today can know. Even if you study so intensely that you arrive at a point where even the Buddhas and Zen masters cannot reach in spite of all their efforts, this will still be a defiled vessel inappropriate for the pure.

Those who are really pure do not even establish purity, so the vessel is not established either. This is why the paths of teacher and apprentice merge. Because there is no obstacle on the way, "you should receive my teaching." Because "it is your fundamental nature," there is nothing to receive from another, nothing to give to anyone.

When you penetrate in this way, then you can be called a teacher, and you can also be called an apprentice. Therefore the disciple climbs over the head of the teacher, and the teacher descends to the feet of the disciple. At this point there is no duality, no discrimination. Therefore the term vessel no longer applies. The disappearance of the vessel in the story represents the realization of this path.

If you reach this state today, it is not your former body and mind, so you cannot even say it encompasses past and present, much less that it is born and dies, comes and goes. Will you keep skin, flesh, bones, and marrow? This is really a state of empty solidity, without inside or outside.

Again I want to illustrate this story with a saying:

If the frosty dawn's bell rings as it's struck,
You never need an empty bowl here.

9

Buddhanandi

When Buddhanandi met the Buddhist master Vasumitra, he said to him, "I have come to discuss meaning with you."

Vasumitra said, "Good man, discussion is not meaning, meaning is not discussion. If you try to discuss meaning, ultimately it is not a meaningful discussion."

Buddhanandi knew that Vasumitra's doctrine was supreme, and he realized the principle of the uncreated.

Buddhanandi was from the state of Kamala. His surname was Gautama. He was extremely eloquent and intelligent.

During his teaching travels, Vasumitra came to Kamala and widely carried out the work of enlightenment. Buddhanandi declared to him, "My name is Buddhanandi, and I want to discuss meaning with you." Vasumitra said, "Good man, discussion is not meaning, meaning is not discussion."

Really true meaning cannot be discussed, and true discussion does not carry any doctrine. Therefore when there is discussion and doctrine, this is not meaningful discussion. That is why Vasumitra said, "If you try to discuss meaning, ultimately it is not a meaningful discussion." In the end there is nothing at all to be considered meaning, nothing at all to be considered discussion.

Even so, "the Buddha does not have two kinds of speech." Therefore seeing the Buddha's body is witnessing the Buddha's tongue. So even if you say that mind and environment are nondual, still this is not true discussion. Thus even if you say there is nothing to say and no principle to reveal, this still does not communicate any meaning. Even if you say nature is reality and mind is absolute, what philosophy is this? And even if you say awareness and objects are both forgotten, still this is not a true statement. Even if awareness and objects are not forgotten, neither is this meaningful. So if you say "guest" and "host," say "one" and "the same," this is increasingly meaningless discussion.

When you arrive here, even to speak of great Manjusri's speechless nonexplanation is not really a true exposition. And even though Vimalakirti stayed silent on his chair, this was not meaningful discussion either. At this point, even Manjusri misapprehended, and Vimalakirti still said "Wrong." Needless to say, Shariputra, foremost among Buddha's disciples in wisdom, and Maudgalyayana, foremost in extraordinary powers, had not yet even dreamed of seeing the meaning of this, like people born blind who had never seen colors.

Furthermore, the Buddha said, "The buddha nature is something unknown to the individually liberated and the self-enlightened." Even universalists of the tenth stage, seeing a flock of cranes from afar, cannot tell if it is water or a flock of cranes. They think it looks like cranes, but still they are not sure. Even these universalists of the tenth stage still do not see the buddha nature clearly. Yet when they realize, through the Buddha's teaching, the existence of inherent essence, they joyfully say, "We have revolved in birth and death for countless eons without discerning this permanence, because we were confused by selflessness."

Furthermore, even if you say you are detached from perception and have forgotten body and mind, have escaped delusion and enlightenment and left behind defilement and purity, you still cannot see this meaning even in a dream. Therefore do not seek in emptiness, do not seek in form. How much less should you seek in Buddhas and Zen masters.

Furthermore, for long eons now how many times have you gone through birth and death, how many times have you come to produce and destroy mind and body? Some may think that this coming and going in birth and death is a dream, an illusion—what a laugh! What kind of talk is this? Is there something that is born and dies, comes and goes, anyway? What would you call the real human body? What do you call dream illusions?

Therefore you should not understand life and death as empty illusions either, nor should you understand them as true reality. If you understand as empty falsehood or true reality, both of these understandings are wrong when you reach here. Therefore, in this one matter, you must search carefully and thoroughly before you will get it. Do not proudly pretend to emptiness and the absolute and consider it the realm of suchness. Even if you understand it as pure and clear as still water, and say it is like the absence of defilement or purity in space, you still cannot understand this point.

Zen master Dongshan, studying with Guishan and Yunyan, suddenly became a peer of myriad things and expounded the Dharma with his whole body, yet something was still not right. Because of this, Yunyan reminded him, "This matter should be taken up carefully." Thus he still had doubts remaining. Taking leave of Yunyan to go elsewhere, as he crossed a river he saw his reflection and immediately realized this matter; thereupon he composed a verse:

> Do not seek from another,
> Or you will be estranged from self.
> I now go on alone,
> Finding I meet It everywhere.
> It now is I,
> I now am not It.
> One should understand in this way
> To merge with suchness as is.

Understanding in this way, Dongshan finally became a successor of Yunyan and the founder of the Dongshan school of Zen. Furthermore, not only did he understand the whole body expounding the Dharma; even though he understood that this is true of everything, every land, every phenomenon, all things in all times expounding the Dharma, there was still a point to which he had not attained.

This is even truer of people today who only understand intellectually. They understand that mind is Buddha, they understand that the body is Buddha, yet they do not understand how the Way of Buddhahood should be—they only see the flowers bloom in spring and the leaves fall in autumn, and think that "all things abide in the normal state." This is laughable. If Buddhism were like this, why would the Buddha have appeared in the world? Why would the founder of Zen have come to China?

From Buddha through the Zen masters of China, there is no distinction in the ranks of the enlightened—all of them attained great awakening. If everyone were a literalist, there would be no enlightened adepts. So when you cast aside literalism to study this point, you can become Buddhas and Zen masters yourselves.

Without great enlightenment and great penetration, you are not on the path of Zen. Therefore one does not abide even in a state of spotless purity, and one does not abide even in a state of empty clarity. This is why an ancient master said, "There should be no traces where you hide, yet you should not hide where there are no traces. In thirty years with my teacher, this is all I learned." This means that spotless purity is not the place to hide, and even if you forget both subject and object you still should not hide here. There is no more past and present to talk about, no delusion or enlightenment to discuss.

When you penetrate in this way, "there are no walls in the ten directions, no gates in the four quarters." Everywhere is free and clear, uncovered and pure. So you should be very thorough; do not be careless.

Today I have a humble saying to explain this story:

Even Manjusri and Vimalakirti could not talk about it,
Even Maudgalyayana and Shariputra could not see it.
If people want to understand the meaning themselves,
When has the flavor of salt ever been inappropriate?

10

Punyamitra

Buddhanandi told Punyamitra, "You are more akin to mind than to your parents, incomparably more akin. When your action accords with enlightenment, this is the mind of all Buddhas. If you seek a formal Buddha externally, it bears no resemblance to you. If you want to know your original mind, it is neither together nor separate."

Hearing this, Punyamitra was greatly enlightened.

Punyamitra was from Magadha. When Buddhanandi came to Magadha in the course of his teaching travels, he saw a white light spring up over Punyamitra's house. He said to his followers, "There must be a saint in this house. He does not speak, but he is a true vessel of the universal vehicle. His feet do not walk upon the ground; he only knows the defilement of contact. He will be my successor."

At that moment, the elder of the house came out and asked, "What do you want?"

Buddhanandi said, "I am looking for an attendant."

The elder said, "I have a son who is already fifty years old but has never spoken a single word and has never set foot on the ground."

Buddhanandi said, "If he is as you say, he is truly my disciple."

When Buddhanandi saw Punyamitra, and Punyamitra heard him say this, Punyamitra suddenly got up and bowed. Then he asked this question: "My father and mother are not my kin; who is most akin? The Buddhas are not my path; whose is the supreme path?"

Buddhanandi replied, "You are more akin to mind than to your parents, incomparably more akin. When your action accords with enlightenment, this is the mind of the Buddhas. If you seek a formal Buddha externally, it bears no resemblance to you. If you want to know your original mind, it is neither together nor separate."

When Punyamitra heard this, he walked seven steps. Buddhanandi said, "This man once met a Buddha and made a universal vow. It was only in consideration of the difficulty of abandoning parental love that he did not speak or walk."

In reality, one's parents are not one's kin, the Buddhas are not one's path. Therefore if you want to know real kinship, it is not to be compared with that of one's parents; if you want to know the real path, it is not to be learned from the Buddhas. The reason for this is that your seeing and hearing do not depend on the eyes and ears of another, your hands and feet do not use the action of another. People are such as they are, and Buddhas are such as they are. If one studies the other, in the end they are not akin—so how could this be considered the path?

Because he maintained this principle, Punyamitra did not say anything or walk anywhere for fifty years. Truly a vessel of the universal vehicle is simply not to be placed in the defilement of contact.

"My parents are not my kin"—these are your words, which thus are akin to your mind. Saying that the Buddhas are not your path, you do not walk—this is your activity that accords with enlightenment. Therefore to seek a formal Buddha outwardly is after all wrong practice.

So the Zen school does not set up words, but only transmits direct pointing, proceeding by means of seeing the essence of mind and realizing enlightenment. Therefore, in causing it to be purely transmitted to let people know it is direct pointing, there is no other model. It is just carried out by having people directly subdue their conceptual faculty and be silent.

This is not a matter of aversion to words or considering silence good; it is to let you know your mind is thus. Like clear water, like space, it is pure, clear, and sparkling clean, harmoniously fluid and unobstructed.

Thus there is nothing revealed outside of one's own mind, there is not a single particle that can veil one's own spirit. The whole being is clear and bright, brighter than pearls and jewels. Even the light of the sun and moon cannot compare to one's own light. Do not compare even the light of a fiery jewel to your own eyes. Have you not heard it said that everyone's light is brighter than a thousand suns shining at once? Those in the dark seek outside, while the illumined do not remain within.

You should contemplate quietly. Within there is nothing to consider akin, outside there is nothing to consider alien.

Even though this is so for all time, do not knock yourself down and pick yourself up. This is why the Zen masters saw each other in person—they just met as such, and there was no big deal besides. This should be clear from this story.

I do not necessarily say it is to be reached by practice and experience, nor that it is to be plumbed by meditative study. I just say that when your mind is completely akin to you, then you are the Path. Outside of this, not seeking a formal Buddha, not seeking a formless Buddha either, in truth we know this—with whom are you together, from whom are you separate? After all it is not a matter of union or separation. Even if you say it is the body, still this is not separate; even if you say it is the mind, still this is not together. Even if you reach this state, do not seek mind outside of body. Even if you come and go in birth and death, this is not the doing of body and mind.

The Buddhas attain enlightenment in all times by maintaining this, and the Zen masters have appeared in India, China, and Japan by maintaining this. You too should maintain this and not consider it beyond you. There is never any error; the causal chain of existence is in fact the turning of the wheel of Buddhism.

When you reach this state, the cycles of existence themselves are the axles of the great vehicle of enlightenment, the karma experienced by living beings is your own livelihood. Even if you say there are sentient and insentient beings, they are just different names for your eyes. Even if you speak of Buddhas and living beings, these are different terms for your mind and intellect. Do not think the mind is superior and the intellect inferior.

In this realm, there are no objects of material sense, no views of mind and phenomena. Therefore everyone is the Path, everything is the mind.

Again I have a humble saying to illustrate this story:

Do not say that words and silence touch upon
The remote and subtle;
How can there be material senses
To defile inherent essence?

11

Parshva

Parshva attended the Buddhist master Punyamitra for three years, never once going to sleep. One day as Punyamitra was reciting a scripture and came to an exposition of the uncreated, Parshva attained enlightenment on hearing it.

Parshva was from central India. His original name was Durjata. On the eve of his birth, his father dreamed of a white elephant with a jeweled seat on its back. On the seat was a bright jewel with a luster that shone upon all the people. When he awoke, Parshva was born.

When Punyamitra came to central India to teach, a certain elder came to him with his son and said to the Buddhist master, "My son here was in the womb for sixty years, so he is named Durjata, 'Difficult Birth.' I have met a wizard who told me that my son is not an ordinary man, but will become a vessel of Buddhism. Now that I have met you, I would have him leave home." So Punyamitra had him shave his head and receive the Buddhist precepts.

Parshva had been in the womb for sixty years and was eighty years old at the time of this meeting, so in all he was one hundred and forty years old when he set out for enlightenment. He was extremely old, so when he set his heart on enlightenment people told him he was too old, that he was unable either to practice meditation or to recite scriptures.

Listening to these critics, Parshva promised himself that he would not lie down as long as he had not mastered the Buddhist canon and attained higher knowledge. So he studied and recited scriptures by day and meditated by night, never going to sleep. He worked diligently for three years, mindless of fatigue, and finally mastered the canon and attained higher knowledge. One day he heard Punyamitra reciting a scripture expounding the uncreated and attained enlightenment.

You should know that he worked diligently in this way, forgetting his fatigue, studying and reciting scripture and practicing meditation, as the work of Buddhas and Zen masters. The master Punyamitra also used to recite scripture and expound the uncreated.

This scripture was a scripture of true universalist Buddhism. Although all the Buddhist scriptures are teachings of the Buddha, he did not recite anything but universalist scriptures and did not rely on anything but scriptures of the complete teaching.

These universalist scriptures do not speak of effacing any sense experience, nor do they talk of removing illusions. The scriptures of the complete teaching not only deal exhaustively with noumenon and the inconceivable, they also deal exhaustively with phenomena. Dealing exhaustively with phenomena means explaining everything from the Buddhas' inspiration to their enlightenment and nirvana, expounding the various vehicles of liberation, and telling about their eras, lands, and names. This is what is meant by complete teaching. So you should know the scriptures of Buddha are like this.

Even if you can say a phrase and understand a principle, if the task of your whole life's study is not finished you can hardly be acknowledged as a Buddha or a Zen master. Thus you should work diligently, forget fatigue, awaken an extraordinary will, and carry out extraordinary practice. Examine thoroughly, investigate completely, continuing day and night. Set your resolve, exert your strength to clearly discern the fundamental meaning of the appearance of enlightened teachers in the world, as well as the import of your own responsibility. If you do this all your life without failing to penetrate every principle and consummate its actualization, then you should be Buddhas and Zen masters.

These days, as the Way of the founding teachings of Zen is neglected, and study has no reality to it, people think it is enough when they understand one word or penetrate one principle. I fear they will be among the conceited. Beware!

Have you not heard it said that the Way is like a mountain, higher as you climb, that virtue is like an ocean, deeper as you enter? Enter the depths and search out the bottom; climb the heights and find the summit. Then for the first time you will be true offspring of the lion.

Do not waste your body and mind. Everyone is a vessel of the Way, every day is a good day. It is just that there are people who have penetrated and people who have not penetrated, depending on whether or not they have carried out careful investigation. It is not necessarily a question of discriminating among people or times either, as the present case attests—Parshva was already over one hundred and forty years old, but because his resolve was single-minded and he worked diligently, mindless of fatigue, ultimately he finished his study in one lifetime.

It is really touching how he spent three years in attendance, without sleeping, in his old age. People these days are lazy, especially when they get old. Thinking far back to the ancient worthies of the distant past, do not consider bitter cold as bitter cold or blistering heat as blistering heat, do not think your physical life will end, do not think your mental powers are insufficient. If you can be like this, you must be one who studies the ancient Way, one who is imbued with the Way. If they study and contemplate the ancients and are imbued with the Way, who would not be Buddhas and Zen masters?

I have already said that he recited scripture. To recite scripture does not necessarily mean that just reciting with your mouth and turning the pages with your hands is actually reciting scripture. Be careful in the house of Buddhas and Zen masters not to waste time in sound and form, not to carry out your activities in the shell of ignorance. When knowledge and wisdom appear everywhere, and the mind ground is always open and clear, this is the way you should "recite scripture." As you practice this way at all times, if you are never dependent, then you will completely realize the uncreated original nature.

Do you not know that we do not come from anywhere even as we are born, and we do not go anywhere even as we die? Born wherever you are, you pass away on the spot; origination and annihilation as time goes by never rest. Therefore birth is not birth, death is not death; and as Zen students, do not keep birth and death hanging on your mind. Do not obstruct yourself by hearing and seeing. Even if it becomes seeing and hearing, becomes sound and form, it is your own storehouse of light.

Emanating light from your eyes, you make arrays of color and form; emanating light from your ears, you hear the buddha work of sounds; emanating light from your hands, you can activate yourself and others; emanating light from your feet, you can walk forward and back.

Again I want to add some humble words to point out this principle:

Turning, turning, how many pages of scripture?
Revolving, revolving, how many scrolls?
Dying here, born there—
Divisions of chapter and verse.

12

Punyayashas

Punyayashas stood before Parshva. Parshva asked him, "Where do you come from?"

Punyayashas said, "My mind is not in movement."

Parshva said, "Where is your abode?"

Punyayashas said, "My mind is not stationary."

Parshva said, "Are you not uncertain?"

Punyayashas said, "The Buddhas were also thus."

Parshva said, "You are not the Buddhas, and the Buddhas also are not so."

Hearing these words, Punyayashas spent three weeks cultivating practice and realized acceptance of the uncreated. He said, "Even the Buddhas are not really so, and neither are you."

Then Parshva accepted him and transmitted the true teaching to him.

Punyayashas was from Kusumapura in Magadha, and his surname was Gautama. When the Buddhist master Parshva first arrived in Kusumapura, he paused to rest under a tree. With his right hand he pointed to the ground and declared to the group, "If this ground turns golden, there will be a sage who will enter the congregation." When he had said this, the earth turned golden in color. Then someone named Punyayashas came and stood before Parshva, as in the story.

Parshva said in verse:

This ground turned gold,
Foretelling the arrival of a sage.
You shall sit at the tree of enlightenment
Where awakening blossoms and becomes complete.

Punyayashas also spoke a verse:

The master sits on golden ground,
Always expounding the real truth,
Turning the light around to illumine the self,
Causing entry into absorption.

Parshva understood what Punyayashas meant, and so he initiated him and transmitted the Buddhist precepts to him.

In the preceding story, Punyayashas was originally a sage, and because of this he said, "My mind is not in motion, my mind is not stationary; the Buddhas are also thus." Yet these are still two views. Why? Because he understood that "my mind is thus" and "the Buddhas are also thus."

Because of this, Parshva "drove off the plowman's ox" and "took away the hungry man's food." Even people who have really found the Way still cannot save themselves completely—why even think of the Buddhas! This is why Parshva said, "You are not the Buddhas." This cannot be known in terms of noumenal essence and cannot be understood in terms of nonform. Therefore it cannot be known by the knowledge of the Buddhas, it cannot be fathomed by one's own perception.

So Punyayashas cultivated practice for three weeks on end after hearing these words, until one day he had a sense of awakening, forgot his own mind, and was liberated from the Buddhas. This is called awakening acceptance of the uncreated. Finally he penetrated this principle, and because there was no inside or outside, he said of his attainment, "Even the Buddhas are not really so, and neither are you."

In reality, the Way of Zen cannot be comprehended in terms of principle, nor understood by mind. Therefore "the body of reality," "the nature of reality," or "myriad things are one mind" cannot be considered ultimate. So it cannot be called the unchanging, and cannot even be understood as purity, much less as empty silence or as the ultimate principle.

Therefore, when they reach this point, the sages of all schools revitalize their original inspiration, reopen the mind ground, directly pass through a way in, and quickly break through their personal views.

This is apparent from the present story. Since Punyayashas was already a sage, when he arrived the ground changed, and the influence of his virtue had the power to awaken people. Nevertheless he still spent three weeks cultivating practice in order to arrive at the point of which I speak. So you should discern clearly, and don't determine the message of Zen based on a little bit of virtue, a little bit of knowledge, personal views, and old feelings. You must be completely thoroughgoing before you can attain it.

Today I have another humble saying to recapitulate:

My mind is not the Buddhas, and not you either;
Coming and going has been here all along.

13

Ashvaghosha

Ashvaghosha asked Punyayashas, "I want to know Buddha—what is it?"

Punyayashas said, "If you want to know Buddha, it is that which does not know."

Ashvaghosha said, "Since Buddha is not knowing, how can one know it is so?"

Punyayashas said, "Not knowing Buddha, how can one know it is not?"

Ashvaghosha said, "This is the meaning of a saw."

Punyayashas said, "That is the meaning of wood."

Punyayashas also asked, "What is the meaning of a saw?"

Ashvaghosha said, "We come out even."

Ashvaghosha also asked, "What is the meaning of wood?"

Punyayashas said, "You are cut apart by me."

At this Ashvaghosha was greatly enlightened.

Ashvaghosha was from Banaras. He was also called by a name meaning Excellence of Virtue, because he excelled in created and un-created virtues. He went to the Buddhist master Punyayashas and first asked, "I want to know Buddha—what is it?" Punyayashas said, "You want to know Buddha? It is what does not know."

Really what one should seek out first in Zen study is the Buddha. All the Buddhas of past, present, and future, and the Zen masters of every generation, are all called people studying Buddha; if they do not study Buddha, they are all called outsiders.

So it is not to be sought by way of sound, not to be sought or perceived by form or signs. Therefore the thirty-two marks of greatness and eighty kinds of refinement are not enough to be considered Buddha. That is why Ashvaghosha asked, "I want to know Buddha— what is it?"

Punyayashas pointed out, "You want to know Buddha? That which does not know is it." That which does not know is none other than Ashvaghosha. Whether before he knew or after he knew, there was no different responsibility, no different appearance. So from ancient times until now it is just thus, sometimes bearing the thirty-two marks of greatness, replete with eighty kinds of refinement, or wearing three heads and eight arms, immersed in the degeneration and misery of the world, sometimes wearing fur and bearing horns, sometimes burdened with fetters and chains, always in the world taking care of one's own actions, appearing and disappearing within one's own mind, wearing different faces.

Therefore, though born, one does not know what it is, and though dying, one does not know what it is. Though you try to assign a form, it is not a thing that can be constructed; though you try to affix a name, it cannot be defined either. Therefore, from eon to eon, totally unknown, it follows and accompanies oneself, yet one does not discern it at all.

Hearing the foregoing story, many interpret it in this way: "When there is any knowing in any way, this goes against buddhahood. When there is no knowing and no discernment, then this must be buddhahood." If you understand this "not knowing" in such a way, why would Punyayashas have taken so much trouble to explain as he did? It is just the same way in going from darkness to darkness—because it is not this way at all, he directly pointed out that "the one not knowing is it."

Ashvaghosha still did not understand what was now indicated to him. Therefore he said, "If the Buddha does not know, how can one know it is so?" Punyayashas retorted, "Not knowing Buddha, how could you know it is not Buddha?" It is not to be sought outside—the one not knowing is Buddha—should one say it is not so?

Then Ashvaghosha said, "This is the meaning of a saw." Punyayashas said, "That is the meaning of wood." Punyayashas again asked, "What is the meaning of a saw?" Ashvaghosha said, "We come out even." Ashvaghosha then asked, "What is the meaning of wood?" Punyayashas said, "You are cut apart by me." At this Ashvaghosha was greatly awakened.

Truly you are thus and I am thus. Opening up fully, Ashvaghosha imparted it with both hands. You and I do not take on a single dot, I and you do not depend on the slightest bit of anything—therefore we come out even, like a two-man saw. Therefore he said, "This is the meaning of a saw."

But Punyayashas said, "That is the meaning of wood." Why? In an endless expanse of darkness, there is no knowledge at all—not a dot is added, not a single bit of knowledge is used. Like a piece of wood, like a pillar, being mindless one is thus. Ultimately there is nowhere to discriminate. Because Ashvaghosha understood this way, Punyayashas said, "That is the meaning of wood."

But with such an understanding Ashvaghosha still had habits remaining and did not know what the teacher meant. At this, Punyayashas went down into the weeds out of compassion and proceeded to ask what he meant by a saw. Ashvaghosha said, "We come out even." Then Ashvaghosha spoke again on his own, asking what Punyayashas meant by wood. Punyayashas again gave him a hand and imparted it to him, saying, "You are cut apart by me."

At this, the paths of teacher and apprentice communed, feelings of past and present were broken; in the middle of a dream he made a road, walking along in emptiness. This is why Punyayashas said, "You are cut apart by me." At this point the frozen bond of mindlessness suddenly melted, and Ashvaghosha left his nest of clarity, greatly opening up to enlightenment.

Punyayashas said to the assembly, "This great man was a king of Vaisali in ancient times. In his country certain people went naked like horses. Using supernatural powers, the king multiplied his body and turned into silkworms so that they could have clothing. That king later was reborn in central India; the horse people, longing for him, cried sadly. Therefore he was called Ashvaghosha, 'Horse Cry.' The Buddha predicted, 'Six hundred years after my death there will be a wise man named Ashvaghosha; refuting the Hindus in Banaras, he will liberate many people. He will liberate countless people and succeed me in transmitting the teaching.' This is now that time." So saying, Punyayashas entrusted to him the Buddha's treasury of the eye of true teaching.

The point of this story should not be wrongly taken to be not knowing anything, where there is no cognition or sense. So even if you are unknowing, see thoroughly and contemplate thoroughly where there is not yet an embryo conceived; even though you look for the Buddha's face or the face of the Zen masters, you cannot find them. Even though you look for human faces, ghosts or animals, you cannot find them.

This is not unchanging, yet it is not moving. It has never been void; there is no question of inside or outside, no separation of absolute and relative. Realize that this truly is your own original face: even if it appears as ordinary or holy, even if it divides into objective and subjective experiences, all comes and goes completely within it, all arises and vanishes herein. It is like the water of the ocean making waves; though they rise again and again, never is any water added. It is also like waves dying away; though they die out and vanish, not a drop is lost.

In the human and celestial realms, this has temporarily come to be called "the Buddhas," come to be called ghosts and animals. It is like temporarily displaying a multitude of faces on one face. If you consider it the face of Buddha, it is not so; and if you consider it the face of a ghost, that is not so either.

Yet the work of teaching has come down through questioning and answering; cultivating phantom meditation, it does buddha work in a dream. Thus the magical arts of teaching in India continue to the present, circulating through India, China, and Japan, turning ordinary people into sages. If you can evolve and practice in this way, then you will not be disappointed by your own faults, and you will not be deluded by your own birth and death. Then you will be real Zennists.

I have another saying to illustrate this story:

The red of the village is not known to the peach blossoms,
Yet they made an ancient Zen master reach certainty.

14

Kapimala

Ashvaghosha, expounding the ocean of buddha nature, said, "The mountains, rivers, and earth are all established on it; all insights and mental powers appear from here."

Hearing this, Kapimala believed and understood it, and was awakened.

Kapimala was from Pataliputra. He used to be a Hindu guru with three thousand followers and was conversant with all the different philosophies.

When Ashvaghosha was teaching in Pataliputra, suddenly an old man collapsed in front of the seat. Ashvaghosha said to the assembly, "This is not an ordinary kind of man; he must have some unusual characteristics." When Ashvaghosha had spoken, the old man disappeared and a golden man sprang up out of the earth. Then he again changed, into a girl; with her right hand she pointed to Ashvaghosha and said in verse:

> I bow to the venerable elder,
> To receive the Buddha's prophecy.
> Now on this land
> The ultimate truth should be spread.

After speaking this verse, she disappeared.

Ashvaghosha said, "There will be a demon who will come to have a contest of power with me." After a while heavy wind and rain came, and the sky and earth were darkened. Ashvaghosha said, "This is evidence of the coming of the demon. I should get rid of it." Then as he pointed into the sky, a huge golden dragon appeared, displayed its awesome power, and caused the mountains to tremble. Ashvaghosha sat still on his seat; the demon's tricks then vanished.

After seven days there was a tiny mite that concealed itself under the preaching seat; Ashvaghosha picked it up in his hand, showed it to the assembly, and said, "This is a transformation of the demon—it is just stealing an audience of my teaching." Then when he let it go, the demon could not move.

Ashvaghosha said to it, "If you would take refuge in the Buddha, the Teaching, and the Community, you would attain supernatural powers." The demon then returned to its original form, bowed, and repented.

Ashvaghosha asked him, "What is your name? How many followers do you have?"

He answered, "My name is Kapimala, and I have three thousand followers."

Ashvaghosha asked, "How is it when you use all your magical power to produce a display?"

Kapimala said, "To produce an ocean is a very small thing for me."

Ashvaghosha said, "Can you produce the ocean of essential nature?"

Kapimala said, "What do you call the ocean of essential nature? I have no knowledge of it."

Ashvaghosha then explained the ocean of essential nature to him, saying, "The mountains, rivers, and earth are all established on it; all insights and mental powers appear from here." Kapimala then believed and understood.

From the time the old man fell on the ground to the time he turned into a mite, he had actually manifested supernatural powers countless times. As he said, to produce an ocean was a small matter for him. But even though he manifested supernatural powers without end, turning oceans into mountains and mountains into oceans, still he did not know even the name of the ocean of essential nature, let alone produce or transform it. Furthermore, since he had no realization of what that is of which the mountains, rivers, and earth are manifestations, Ashvaghosha explained that they are transformations of the ocean of essential nature. Not only that, all insights and psychic powers are manifested from this.

Immeasurable states of concentration such as the Heroic March, in which one can enter any state at will, and the supernormal faculties such as clairvoyance, clairaudience, and so on, have no beginning and no end. This is what is meant by the saying, "Three times three in front, three times three in back." Just when this establishes the mountains, rivers, and earth, concentration transmutes into earth, water, fire, and air, and also into mountains, rivers, plants, and trees. It also turns into skin, flesh, bones, and marrow, and also into body and limbs. Not a single thing, not a single phenomenon, has ever come from outside.

Thus there is no wasted time or effort twenty-four hours a day, no appearance of countless births and deaths in vain. Therefore seeing has no limit, hearing has no limit either; such seeing and hearing perhaps not even buddha knowledge can assess. Is this not produced of the ocean of essential nature?

Thus everything, every particle, is boundless reality and does not come within the scope of number or measure at all. This is the ocean of essential nature; that is why it is thus.

Furthermore, to see the body now is to see the mind; to know the mind is to realize the body. There is no duality at all in mind and body; how could you divide essence and characteristics?

Even if Kapimala manifested miracles in a non-Buddhist way, while this is not beyond possibility, still he did not know himself that this is the ocean of essential nature. Because of this he was confused about himself and doubted others. Moreover, since he did not know all existences, he was not at all one who had arrived at the root. When he matched powers, he lost, so ultimately his demonic powers were exhausted and he could not produce any more wonders. Finally he gave up his ego and became Ashvaghosha's disciple, ceasing contention and revealing what is right.

So even if you understand the mountains, rivers, and earth, do not get uselessly tied up in sound and form. Even if you clarify your own original nature, still do not dwell in conscious knowledge. Yet conscious knowledge too is one or two faces of Buddha, of Zen mastery: as we say, "Walls and shards are It."

The original nature is not bound by perception or knowledge; it does not depend on movement or stillness. But when the ocean of nature is established, of course movement and stillness, coming and going, after all never cease—they appear simultaneously with skin, flesh, bones, and marrow.

If you talk about the root basis, even appearing as seeing and hearing, appearing as sound and form, there is nothing to do for another. So when you strike space it echoes, and thus all sounds are manifested; transforming emptiness to manifest myriad things is why shapes and forms are so various.

Therefore you should not think that emptiness has no form, or that emptiness has no sound. When you furthermore investigate carefully on reaching this point, it cannot be considered void and it cannot be considered existent either. Therefore it is not to be considered something in concealment or revelation, or something with selfhood and otherhood.

What do you call other, what do you call self? This is like space, where there is not a single thing, like the ocean, where all waters appear. Throughout all time, it has never changed; how could going and coming have separate roads?

Therefore, revelation adds nothing and concealment causes no loss. The conglomeration of many elements forms this body. Obliterating myriad things, we go on to speak of one mind. Therefore understanding the Way and realizing the mind should not be sought externally at all.

But if the scenery of your own original ground just becomes manifest, others call this a human face, or a ghost, or an animal. An ancient Zen master said, "If you want to understand this matter, here I am like an ancient mirror; when a foreigner comes a foreigner is reflected, when a native comes a native is reflected."

This is all magical concentration, so it has no beginning or ending limits. Therefore, when it establishes the mountains, rivers, and earth, it all depends on this; manifesting insights and powers too depends on this. So you should not see even an inch of the whole earth as being outside your own mind. Do not put even a drop of river water outside the ocean of nature.

Again I would like to add a humble saying:

Even if the enormous waves flood the skies,
When has the water of the pure ocean ever changed?

15

Nagarjuna

When Kapimala answered the invitation of the Naga king, he received a wish-fulfilling jewel. Nagarjuna asked, "This is the ultimate jewel of the world; does it have form, or is it formless?"

Kapimala said, "You only know of having form or not; you do not know that this jewel neither has form nor is formless. And you do not yet know that this jewel is not a jewel."

Hearing this, Nagarjuna was profoundly enlightened.

Master Nagarjuna was a man of western India. He was known by the names Dragonic Ferocity and Supreme Dragon. In his time, Kapimala, having been ordained and having received the transmission of Buddhism, came to western India. There was a prince there who respected the name of the Buddhist master Kapimala and invited him to his palace and presented him with offerings.

Kapimala said, "The Buddha has a teaching that monks should not approach the houses of kings, ministers, and politicians."

The prince said, "North of our capital city is a huge mountain, in which there is a stone cave. Would the master meditate in peace there?"

Kapimala agreed. When he had gone a couple of miles into the mountains, he encountered a huge python. Kapimala went straight ahead, paying no attention to it, but the python came and finally encircled the Buddhist master. Kapimala then administered Buddhist initiation to the snake, and it left.

As Kapimala was about to reach the cave, an old man dressed in white came out to greet him. Kapimala asked him where he lived, and the old man said, "In former times when I was a monk I very much enjoyed quietude, and lived alone in the mountain forests. There was a novice monk who used to come and ask for instruction, and I, feeling it troublesome to reply, produced thoughts of anger and resentment. After I died I became a python and have lived in this cave for a thousand years. Now that I have chanced to meet you and gotten to hear the initiatory teachings, I have just come to thank you."

Kapimala then asked who else was living in those mountains. The python said, "Several miles north of here there is a great man named Nagarjuna who always preaches to a crowd of Nagas. I also listen."

Kapimala finally went there with his followers. Nagarjuna came out and greeted the Buddhist master, saying, "The deep mountains are lonely and desolate, a place where Nagas dwell. Why have you, a great sage, a supremely honorable one, bent your steps here?"

Kapimala said, "I am not the supremely honorable one. I have come to visit this wise man."

Nagarjuna thought silently, "Has this teacher attained certainty and clearly illumined the eye of enlightenment? Is he a great sage continuing the true Way?"

Kapimala said, "Even though you are speaking in your heart, I already know it in my mind. Just take care of renunciation of wordly ties—why worry about whether I am a sage or not?"

Hearing this, Nagarjuna repented and became a renunciate. Kapimala ordained him, and the community of Nagas also received the Buddhist precepts.

After that, Nagarjuna followed Kapimala for four years. Kapimala answered an invitation of the Naga king, who presented him with a precious wish-fulfilling jewel. Nagarjuna then initiated the dialogue about the ultimate jewel and was finally deeply enlightened.

Nagarjuna had studied different paths and had supernormal powers. He often went to the palace of the Nagas and read the scriptures of the seven prehistorical Buddhas. As soon as he saw the title he would immediately know the heart of the scripture. He always taught a group of five hundred Nagas.

The Naga kings Nanda, Bhadrananda, and others were all enlightened beings; they had all received the bequest of the former Buddhas and kept their scriptures in storage. Now that the affinity of humanity with the scriptural teachings of the great Shakyamuni Buddha is virtually exhausted, all of them should be stored in the Naga palace.

Even though Nagarjuna had such great powers and used to converse with the great Naga kings, he still was not a truly enlightened man—he was just studying outside paths. Only after he became the disciple of the Buddhist master Kapimala did he have the wide-open clear eye. So everyone thinks that Nagarjuna was not only a Zen ancestor, he was also the ancestor of various schools. The Shingon school also considers him an original patriarch, the Tendai school also considers him an ancestor, and so do diviners and silk growers and others.

The fact is that although he learned all the arts in the past, after he had become a Buddhist master the disciples he abandoned still considered Nagarjuna as their own predecessor. These are demons and animals who mix up the true and the false and do not distinguish jewels from pebbles. When it comes to Nagarjuna's Buddhist teaching, only Kanadeva got the true transmission—the rest were all schools that he had abandoned. This can be known from the present story.

Nagarjuna asked, "This jewel is the ultimate treasure of the world; does it have form, or is it formless?" In reality, Nagarjuna knew to begin with. Do you consider it to have form? Do you consider it formless? He was clinging uncertainly to the views of existence and nonexistence; that is why Kapimala taught him as he did.

Actually, even if it is a worldly jewel, when you talk about its true reality it is not formed or formless—it is just a jewel. Moreover, the jewel stuck in the wrestler's forehead, the jewel in the king's topknot, the Naga king's jewel, and the jewel inside the drunken man's robe— scriptural metaphors for inherent buddha nature—are not within the view of others, so it is difficult to discern whether or not they have form. Yet these jewels are all mundane jewels, not the ultimate jewel of the Way. Needless to say he could not know this jewel is not even a jewel. Truly we must be careful.

Zen master Xuansha said, "The whole body is a jewel—who would you inform?" He also said, "The whole universe is a single bright jewel." Really this cannot be discerned by human views. Even though it be a mundane jewel, it does not come from outside—all appears from people's own minds.

Therefore Indra, king of gods, used it as a wish-fulfilling jewel. When sick, if you apply this jewel to the ailing part the sickness disappears. When troubled, if you put this jewel on your head the trouble spontaneously disappears. Supernatural powers and magical displays also depend on this jewel.

Among the seven treasures of a ruling monarch there is a wish-fulfilling jewel from which all rare treasures are born. Its use is infinite. In this way there are differences according to the ordinary and higher psychological states of human experience.

The wish-fulfilling jewel of the human world is also called a grain of rice. This is called a precious gem. Compared to the jewels in the heavens, this is considered artificial, yet it is called a jewel. Moreover, when Buddhism dies out, the relics of Buddha will become wish-fulfilling jewels raining everywhere; they will also become grains of rice to help people.

Even if it appears as a Buddha body, as grains of rice, as myriad phenomena, or as a single jewel, as one's own mind manifests it becomes a body five feet tall, it becomes a three-headed figure, it becomes a body wearing fur and horns, it becomes all kinds of forms. So then you should discern that mind jewel.

Do not live secluded in mountain forests seeking peace and quiet like that ancient monk. Really this is a mistake that has been made in the past, and in recent times also, by those who have not yet realized enlightenment. Still people say that mixing with others, studying in all activities, is not tranquil, so they want to live alone in the mountain forests and quietly sit in meditation to carry out the Way. Those who say this and then hide in the mountains, practicing wrongly, mostly get into aberrations because of this. If you want to know why, it is because they do not know reality and they vainly put themselves first.

People like this say, "Zen master Damei sat among the pines and mist with a miniature shrine on his head; Zen master Guishan also practiced in the clouds and mists with tigers and wolves for companions. We too should practice this way." This is really laughable. You should know that the ancients practiced this way while awaiting appropriate conditions to teach, in order to mature their work on the Way after having become enlightened and received the approval of a true teacher. Damei received the true seal of Mazu, and Guishan received the transmission of Baizhang—it was after their enlightenment that they lived alone in the mountains, it was not what the ignorant envision.

People of ancient times like Yinshan and Luoshan did not live alone before they had attained enlightenment. They were real people who had realized the Way, great sages with clear eyes, whose virtuous conduct was great in their time, and who left their fame to latter ages. If you live in the mountains while neglecting to investigate what you should investigate and failing to arrive where you should arrive, you will be like monkeys. This is a serious lack of the spirit of the Way.

If people just practice to train themselves, they become followers or conditionally enlightened; they will become spoiled seed for naught. Spoiled seed means they are scorched seed, in that they cut off the seed of buddhahood.

Therefore, after you have practiced Zen carefully and thoroughly in a community, having studied with one who knows for a long time, when the great matter is thoroughly clear and you have just about finished clarifying and mastering yourself, you may say that deepening the roots and strengthening the stems for a while is the teaching imparted by the ancient masters. But Dogen, the founder of our Zen school, proscribed living alone. This was to prevent people from aberration. His successor Ejo said, "My disciples should not live alone. Even if you have attained the Way, you should cultivate and refine it in a community. Needless to say, those who are still studying should not live alone. Anyone who goes against this rule is not a member of my school."

Zen master Yuanwu also said, "After they had attained the essence of Zen, the ancients would live in the mountains for ten or twenty years, forgetting all about human society, forever forsaking the realm of dust. In these times we cannot presume to aspire to this."

Huanglong Huinan said, "Rather than grow old in the mountain forests preserving the Way by yourself, is it not better to guide people in a community?"

The great Zen masters of recent eras have all disapproved of living alone. Especially since people's faculties and capacities are all inferior to those of ancient times, they should just stay in communities to practice, refine, and master the Way. Even one of the ancients was so heedless that he wrongly indulged in peace and quiet to the extent that when a new student came to ask him for help, he did not reply when he should have, getting angry instead. So we know that his body and mind were not yet harmonized. If you live alone apart from your teacher, even if you can preach like Nagarjuna, you will still be making some kind of retribution for your actions.

You have been able to hear the right teaching of Buddha because you have planted roots of goodness. The teaching says not to approach kings and politicians, but do not therefore wish to live alone unencumbered. Just progress diligently on the work of the Way, and single-mindedly pierce through the source of the Dharma. This is the real teaching of the Buddha.

Today I have a humble saying to bring out the preceding story:

The solitary light, aware space, is always free from darkness;
The wish-fulfilling jewel distributes its shining radiance.

16

Kanadeva

Kanadeva visited the great master Nagarjuna. Knowing he was a man of wisdom, Nagarjuna sent an attendant out to place a bowl full of water in front of Kanadeva just as the latter was about to reach the gate. Nagarjuna then watched to see what Kanadeva would do. Kanadeva placed a needle on the surface of the water and brought it with him to meet Nagarjuna. Happily they had a meeting of minds.

Kanadeva was from southern India. He used to perform rituals for good fortune, propitiatory rites for blessings; he also enjoyed philosophy, rhetoric, and debate.

In the course of his teaching travels after having attained Buddhist enlightenment, Nagarjuna came to southern India. Many people there believed in performing rites for blessings. Hearing Nagarjuna explain the subtle truth for them, they said to one another, "For people to have done things to merit blessings is what is most important in the world. He talks nonsense about 'enlightened nature,' but who can see this nature?"

Nagarjuna said, "Do you want to see the enlightened nature? First you must get rid of your conceit."

They said, "Is the enlightened nature large or small?"

Nagarjuna said, "The enlightened nature is not large or small, not wide or narrow. It has no blessing, no retribution; it is undying and unborn."

Seeing how superior his doctrine was, they all changed their minds.

A man of great knowledge among them, Kanadeva, visited Nagarjuna, and they ultimately attained accord. Then Nagarjuna shared the teaching seat with him just as Gautama Buddha had done with Kasyapa on Spiritual Mountain. Nagarjuna then expounded the teaching for them by manifesting the form of the full moon. Master Kanadeva said to the crowd, "This is the teacher manifesting the essential form of the enlightened nature to show us. How do we know? Because signless, formless absorption is like the full moon; the meaning of the buddha nature is wide-open clarity." When Kanadeva had finished speaking, the sphere disappeared; reappearing, Nagarjuna spoke the following verse:

Body manifests the full moon symbol
To represent the body of all Buddhas.
The teaching has no such shape;
Thereby we discern it is not sound or form.

Thus teacher and apprentice were indistinguishable and the lifeline flowed through.

The foregoing event is not ordinary. Kanadeva united with the Way at the very first: Nagarjuna did not have a word of explanation, and Kanadeva did not have a word of inquiry. Therefore the existence of "teacher" and "apprentice" could hardly be maintained—how could "guest" and "host" be distinguished?

Thereafter Kanadeva especially upheld and expounded the religious way, and eventually it was known throughout India as the Deva school. It was, as it is said, like "piling snow in a silver bowl, hiding a heron in the moonlight."

Because it was like this, when they first saw each other a bowl full of water was immediately placed before the seat—could inside and outside exist? Since it was a full bowl, there was no lack. This is also still water, absolutely clear, pure throughout. Expansive, filling, it is aware and radiant. Therefore Kanadeva put a needle on the water and met with understanding.

It is necessary to reach the very bottom and the very top. There is no absolute or relative. Reaching this point, teacher and apprentice can hardly be distinguished: when you array them, they're not the same; when you mix them together, there are no traces.

This matter is manifested by the raising of eyebrows and blinking of eyes; this matter is shown by seeing color and hearing sound. Therefore there is nothing to name sound and color, no seeing or hearing to abandon. Round and bright, without form, it is like the transparency of clear water. It is like penetrating through the spiritual noumenon and seeking the spiritual sword. The point appears everywhere; clear and bright, it pervades the mind. Water too pierces mountains with its flow and inundates the skies; and a needle penetrates a bag and pierces a seed. Yet water is after all not destroyed by anything—how could there be any tracks made in it? And a needle, to other things, is harder than a diamond.

Are this needle and water anything else but your body and mind? When swallowing up, it is just a needle; when spitting out, it is clear water. Therefore the paths of teacher and apprentice arrive together, fulfilled together, there being no self or other at all. Therefore, when the lifeline goes right through and there is open clarity, it cannot be hidden in the ten directions; it is like squash vines entwining squashes—they cling and entwine—it is just that there is only one's own mind.

Furthermore, even if you have gotten to know the clear water, you should feel it carefully and clearly realize there is a needle in it. If you drink it by mistake, it will cut your throat.

Yet even though it be so, do not entertain a dualistic understanding. Just swallow up, spit out, and think carefully and thoroughly. Even if you feel clear and pure, empty and fluid, right then there must be a pervading firmness—the disasters of water, fire, and wind cannot impinge upon it, nor will the eons of becoming, subsistence, decay, and emptiness affect it.

I have another humble saying to explain this story:

One needle fishes all the waters of the ocean;
Wherever it goes, the ferocious dragon can hardly conceal its
    body.

17

Rahulata

In attendance on Kanadeva, Rahulata experienced enlightenment on hearing about a past cause.

Rahulata was from Kapilavastu. As for the past cause, after Kanadeva had been liberated and was traveling around teaching, he came to Kapilavastu; there was a rich man there named Brahmashuddhaguna, in whose garden a fungus grew on a tree one day, a fungus like a mushroom, with an exceedingly fine flavor. Only the elder and his second son Rahulata partook of it. After they ate it, it regrew, and when it was gone it sprouted again. Yet the other members of the family could not see it. At that time, Kanadeva knew the past cause of this phenomenon, and he went to that house. The elder asked him the reason, and Kanadeva said, "In your house once in the past you gave offerings to a monk, and that monk's perception of the Way was not yet clear. Because he was receiving alms in vain, he became a tree fungus to repay. Since only your son and you provide offerings with pure sincerity, you have been able to partake of it, not so the others."

Kanadeva also asked the elder how old he was. The man said he was seventy-nine years old. Kanadeva then spoke a verse:

Entering the Way, if one does not penetrate truth,
One returns one's body to requite the alms of the faithful.
When your years are eighty-one,
The tree will not grow ears.

After hearing this verse, the rich man was even more respectful. He said, "I am old and feeble and unable to serve you, but please let me give up my second son to follow you as a renunciate." Kanadeva said, "The Buddha prophesied the appearance of this child; he said that in the second five hundred years there would be a great master of the teaching. Our meeting now is the fulfillment of a past cause." Then Kanadeva shaved Rahulata's head, and Rahulata eventually became a Zen master.

In ancient and modern times, this story has often been brought up to admonish students who vainly mix in with the pure flow without shame or conscience, who wastefully accept the charity of the faithful without having any knowledge or discernment. Really one should be ashamed of this. As monks we have abandoned home and entered the Way—even our dwelling place is not our land, and what we eat is not ours at all, what we wear is not earned by our own labor. Not even a drop of water or a blade of grass is to be exploited. Why? Because you people are all born and raised by the land, and all the land and waters in the country belong to the sovereign. Therefore, if you live at home you serve your parents, and if you work for the nation you serve the ruler. At such a time heaven and earth give protection, and you naturally receive the benefit of the sun and shade energies. So if you make a halfhearted claim to seek the Buddha's teaching, and don't serve your parents and rulers as you should serve them, how will you requite the debt of gratitude to your parents who bore and raised you, and to the sovereign, the rivers, and the earth? If you enter the Way but do not have the eye of the Way, if you do not have enlightened vision, you should be called thieves, plunderers of the country.

You say you have already abandoned sentiment, entered nondoing, and left the world, so after having become mendicants you don't pay respects to your parents or civil leaders. Having adopted the guise of Buddhists, you rest your bodies in the pure stream. Even though you say you receive that which is given by women and children, this is not the same as receiving it while in ordinary life—it is alms given in faith. And as an ancient said, if your eye of enlightenment is not yet clear it is hard to chew through even a single grain of rice, but when your eye of enlightenment is clear and bright, even if you had space for a bowl and a mountain of rice, even if you partook of it every day and night, you would not be beholden to the faithful for their alms. But you don't pay attention to whether or not your eye of enlightenment is complete. Having become mendicants in the wrong way, you think you will receive offerings from people, and if offerings are scarce you look to humanity in vain.

Think about it—when you left home and parted from your native places, you hadn't a grain of provisions stored, and you weren't wearing a single thread: you roamed alone and exposed. You should just devote your body to the purpose of the eye of truth and give up your body for the purpose of the Way. Should beginning aspirants vainly do anything for the sake of fame and profit, or for food and clothing?

So it is not necessary to ask about others—just look back on your very first determination of mind; look into yourself and see what is right and what is not right. This is why it is said that it is hard to be as careful of the end as of the beginning. If they would really be as beginners, who would not become people of the Way?

Thus, even though they all become monks and nuns, people uselessly become plunderers of the nation. How is that so? The monk of ancient times in the present story requited his debt by not regressing in practice even though his eye of enlightenment was not yet clear. Thus he even became a tree mushroom for this reason. As for the likes of monks nowadays, when your one life is about to end, the king of death cannot release you. Today's gruel and rice may become molten iron or iron pills, and when you ingest them your body and mind will be inflamed.

Zen master Yunfeng Yue said, "Haven't you heard how one of our spiritual ancestors said, 'Having entered the Path, if you don't penetrate the principle you should turn over your body to pay back the donations of the faithful.' This is something definitely certain, ultimately not false. Elders, be careful of time—time doesn't wait for anyone. Don't wait until the morning when the light of your eyes falls to the ground and you begin to die. If you don't have a sieve's worth of accomplishment in the field of monkhood, you'll fall into the pains of a hundred punishments, enclosed by iron mountains. Don't say I didn't tell you."

Good people, we have been lucky enough to meet the true teaching of Buddha. This is more rare than meeting a tiger in the middle of a city. It is supposed to be rarer yet than the single blooming of the udumbara flower, which blooms once in three thousand years. Concentrating carefully and investigating thoroughly, you need the eye of the Way to be pure and clear.

Don't you see today's story? Don't say "sentient" and "insentient," don't divide into objective and subjective. The monk of a former life had become the wood fungus of today. When it was a mushroom it didn't know it had been a monk, and when he was a monk he didn't know he had appeared as myriad things. So now as a sentient being he has a little cognitive awareness.

But though he has some sense of discernment, he is still not different from a wood mushroom. Why? The mushroom's not knowing you is ignorance, is it not? Your not knowing the mushroom is just the same. Because of this there is distinction between the animate and inanimate, the sentient and insentient, there are distinctions in subjective and objective states. When you clarify yourself, what would you call animate and what inanimate? It is not past, future, or present; not senses, objects, or consciousness. There is no one to stop and nothing stopped either, no self-doing and no other-doing. You should really investigate very thoroughly and see it with body and mind shed.

Don't vainly be proud of having become a monk in form; don't wrongly stop at having left the ordinary household. Even if you avoid the flood, you'll be bothered by the fire. Even if you break away from mundane turmoil, it is still unavoidable even in buddhahood—so how much the more so for those who are not like this, who pursue things and are confused by others, who are like light hairs or floating dust, running east and west, rising and falling to court and country, their feet not walking on real ground, their hearts not having arrived at truth. Such people not only cheat away one life, they will go on passing ages in vain.

Don't you know that from ancient times until now there has never

been error, there has been no obstruction? You don't yet know of it—
that is why you become floating dust for naught. If you do not finish
today, until when will you wait?

I have a humble saying to expound the foregoing story:

What a pity the eye of the Way is not clear—
Losing himself, repaying others, his retribution isn't ended.

18

Sanghanandi

Sanghanandi's mind was opened when he heard Rahulata say to him in verse,

Because I no longer have self,
You should see my self;
Since you take me as your teacher,
Know that I am not my self.

Master Sanghanandi was the son of King Ratnavyuha of Shravasti. He was able to speak as soon as he was born. He always praised Buddhist works. When he was seven years old he was already weary of the pleasures of the world, and declared to his parents, "I bow to my great loving father, and salute my bone and blood mother: I now want to leave home, and hope for your compassion."

But his parents sternly forbade him to leave home. In protest, he stopped eating, so then they allowed him to become a monk while staying at home. They also had a monk become his teacher. For nineteen years he never regressed or flagged in his efforts, but he thought to himself, "Living physically in the royal palace, how can I be considered a mendicant, a leaver of home?"

One night a celestial light shone down; he happened to see an even road, and unconsciously began to walk slowly on it. After a few miles he came to the front of a huge cliff. There was a cave there, in which he rested peacefully.

His father the king, having lost his son, cast out the monk who was teaching him, sending him out of the country to look for his son. The monk was unable to find Sanghanandi.

Ten years later the Buddhist master Rahulata came to Shravasti on his teaching journeys. There was a river there called Golden Waters, the taste of its water exceptionally fine. The images of the five meditation Buddhas appeared in midstream, and Rahulata said to his group, "At the source of this river, about five hundred miles away, there lives a sage named Sanghanandi. The Buddha predicted that a thousand years after his death Sanghanandi would succeed to the ranks of the saints."

So saying, Rahulata led his students upriver, and there they found Sanghanandi sitting peacefully in a state of concentration. The Buddhist master and his group watched him, and after twenty-one days he finally arose from stillness.

Rahulata asked Sanghanandi, "Is your body stabilized or is your mind stabilized?" He replied, "Body and mind are both stabilized." Rahulata said, "If the body and mind are both stabilized, how is it that there are exit and entry?"

Indeed, if you say body and mind are both stable, how can there be exit and entry? If you cultivate stability in body and mind, this is still not true stability. If it is not true stability, it will have exit and entry, and if it has exit and entry, it cannot be said to be stable. Don't seek body and mind in stabilization. Zen study is basically the shedding of body and mind. What do you call body, what do you call mind?

Sanghanandi said, "Even though there is exit and entry, the character of stability is not lost. It is like gold in a well; the substance of the gold is always still."

Rahulata said, "If there is no movement or stillness in the gold being in the well or out of the well, what goes out and in? That is, if gold has movement and stillness, and has a place to come out and a place to go in, this is not real gold.

Still not understanding this principle, Sanghanandi said, "You say the gold moves or is still, what thing comes out and goes in—you concede the movement and stillness of the gold, yet gold is not movement or stillness." If you say the gold has no movement or stillness but has exit and entry, there is still a dualistic view.

Therefore Rahulata said, "If the gold is in the well, what comes out is not gold; if the gold is out of the well, what is in there?" Outside after all doesn't let in, and inside doesn't let out. When emerging, emerging completely, when entering, entering completely, why be in or out of a well? That is why Rahulata said, "What comes out is not gold—what is in there?"

Not comprehending this principle, Sanghanandi said, "If the gold comes out of the well, what is in the well is not gold. If the gold is in the well, what comes out is not a thing." These words are actually ignorant of the nature of gold, so Rahulata said Sanghanandi was not right. Though it seemed he was really in stable concentration and perceived this principle, yet Sanghanandi still had views of things and self. That is why I say the principle wasn't clear to him, and there is no truth to this as doctrine—it's like a light hair following the wind.

Because it is not really true, Rahulata said, "This doctrine must fall." He was talking about what Sanghanandi had said.

Sanghanandi said, "That doctrine doesn't stand."

Out of compassion, Rahulata said again, "Because your point doesn't stand, my point is made."

But because he understood selflessness wrongly, Sanghanandi said, "Though 'my doctrine' is established, it is because things are not self."

Rahulata said, "My point is already made, because 'I' have no 'self.'"

Although Sanghanandi knew that all things are really selfless, still he didn't know reality, so he said, "Because self is selfless, what doctrine or point can you establish?"

In order to let you know personally, Rahulata said, "Because 'I' have no self, your point is established."

The physical elements are really not oneself; mind and body are originally not existent. Realizing somewhat on reflection that there is self where there is no self, Sanghanandi said, "What sage taught you to realize this selflessness?"

To let him know that the path of teacherhood and discipleship is not arbitrary, Rahulata said, "I learned to realize this selflessness from my teacher Kanadeva, the Buddhist master."

Sanghanandi said, "I bow to Kanadeva, who produced you. Since you are selfless, I want to have you for my teacher."

Rahulata said, "Since I have no self, you should see my self. Since you take me as a teacher, know that I am not my self."

Those who manage to see the real self no longer keep the subjective self, so how can anything block their eyes? Perception and cognition are ultimately not differentiated; there is one thing, one reality, which is undivided. Therefore the paths of teacher and apprentice meet with no separation between sages and ordinary people. When you see this principle, you are said to meet the Buddhas and Zen masters. Therefore you make your self the teacher, and make the teacher your self—they cannot be split apart.

Sanghanandi suddenly realized this principle, so he sought initiation and liberation. Rahulata said, "Your mind is free, not to be tied down by me."

When the Buddhist master Rahulata had spoken, he lifted a golden bowl all the way up to the palace of Brahma, took fragrant rice from there, and offered it to the group. The people in his group, however, suddenly became disgusted. Rahulata said, "This is not my fault—it is your own doing." Then he had Sanghanandi sit next to him and share the food.

The people thought this was strange. Rahulata said, "This is the reason you don't get any food. The one sitting with me is a past Buddha who has come down to be reincarnated out of compassion. You people, on the other hand, reached the third realization in a past eon, but still have not experienced noncontamination."

The people said, "We have to believe in your supernormal powers, but we doubt that he was a past Buddha."

Knowing the people were contemptuous, Rahulata said, "When

the Buddha was alive, the world was even, without hills, and the waters of the rivers and canals were sweet; plants and trees flourished, the land was rich, there was no misery, and people behaved virtuously. Eight centuries after the Buddha's death, the world is hilly, the trees are withered, people lack sincere faith, right recollection is weak—they don't believe in reality, but only like magical powers."

So saying, he extended his hand gradually and reached into the earth down to the sphere of adamant, where he took some ambrosial water and brought it to the meeting place in a crystal bowl. Everyone was humbled and repented of their error when they saw this.

How sad it is that it was already like this eight centuries after the Buddha—how much more acute it is now, in the last five hundred years of the teaching, when even though the name of Buddhism is heard, it is not understood what its principles might be. Because there are no bodies and minds that have arrived at it, no one asks how it should be. Even having intelligence and having a little perception and comprehension due to the teachings of the Buddha, one may be invaded by laziness and have no real faith or understanding. Therefore, when there are no true people of the Way, there is no resolve. Truly, because of the moral weakness and longstanding ill effects of doings of the final age, we have met with such a time as this. It is more than a shame.

But even though we are pitiful both as teacher and students, not having been born in the ages of the true or at least the imitation teaching, you should consider how Buddhism gradually spread eastward, reaching its final age, and in our country we have heard the true teaching of the Buddha for fifty or sixty years. This event should be considered the beginning.

Buddhism flourishes wherever it goes. You people should arouse your determination with bold and powerful effort, not consider your selves as yourselves, directly realize selflessness. Promptly become mindless, and without being constrained by the doings of body and mind, without being bound by feelings of confusion or enlightenment, without staying in the cave of birth and death, without being tied up in the net of sentient beings and Buddhas, you should know that there is a self which never changes through all time.

As a capping phrase, I say:

Mental workings turn freely in accord with mental
    characteristics;
How many times has the self of selves changed faces now?

19

Jayashata

Jayashata attended the Buddhist master Sanghanandi. Once when they heard the sound of the wind blowing in the chimes in the hall, Sanghanandi asked Jayashata, "Is it the chimes ringing or the wind ringing?" Jayashata said, "It is neither the wind nor the chimes—it is just my mind ringing." Sanghanandi said, "And who is the mind?" Jayashata said, "Because all is silent." Sanghanandi said, "Good! Who but you would succeed to my path?" Then he transmitted the treasury of the teaching to Jayashata.

Jayashata was born seven days after his mother became pregnant, having dreamed of a great spirit holding a mirror. His skin was lustrous as crystal, and he was naturally fragrant and clean without even being washed. Since the time he was born, a round mirror always appeared accompanying the boy. He was always fond of peace and quiet, and was not at all influenced by mundane conditions. As for this mirror, when the boy sat it was right in front of him, and all the works of past and present Buddhas appeared in it. It was even clearer than illumining his mind with the teachings of the Buddha. When the boy went anywhere this mirror followed him like a halo, yet the boy's form was not concealed. When the boy lay down, the mirror covered the bed like a celestial canopy. The mirror followed him whatever he did.

Now when Sanghanandi, who was traveling around teaching,

came to the land where Jayashata lived, a cool breeze suddenly came over his group, and their minds and bodies were extraordinarily delighted, although they didn't know why. Sanghanandi said, "This is the breeze of enlightened virtue; a sage will appear in the world and inherit the lamp of the masters."

Having said this, Sanghanandi used his supernormal powers to take his group over the mountains and valleys. In a short time they reached the base of a peak, and he said to the group, "On the summit of this peak there is a canopy of purple clouds—there must be a sage living here." Then they wandered around for a long time.

Finally they saw a mountain hut, and a boy holding a round mirror came right up to Sanghanandi. Sanghanandi asked him, "How old are you?" He answered, "A hundred years old." Sanghanandi said, "You're still a child—why do you say you're a hundred years old?" The boy said, "I don't understand the reason—I'm just a hundred years old, that's all." Sanghanandi said, "Are you fulfilling your potential?" He answered, "The Buddha said, 'Even if someone lives for a hundred years, if he doesn't understand the potential of enlightenment, it is not as good as living one day while definitely realizing this.'"

Sanghanandi said, "What does the thing in your hands represent?"

The boy said, "The great round mirror of the Buddhas: flawless and unclouded inside and out, two people both can see, their minds and eyes alike."

When his parents heard this, they let the boy leave home. Master Sanghanandi brought him back to his place, invested him with the Buddhist precepts, and named him Jayashata. The round mirror suddenly disappeared when the boy left home.

Actually everyone's light is just like this round mirror, without flaw or obscurity inside and outside. Ever since the boy was born he always praised buddha works and did not mix in mundane affairs. Looking into the clear mirror, he observed the deeds of Buddhas past and present. Though he really knew that their minds and eyes are all like each other, still he thought he did not understand the potential of the Buddhas, so he said he was a hundred years old.

If you understand the potential of Buddhas, the potential of enlightenment, even for only one day, this not only surpasses a hundred years, it also surpasses innumerable lifetimes. Therefore he finally gave up the round mirror.

Through this story it should be known that the work of the Buddhas is not done carelessly and is not easy. When you understand the great round mirror of the Buddhas, could there be anything else left over?

Nevertheless this is still not the real thing. How could there even be the round mirror of the Buddhas? How could two people both realize it? What inner and outer flawlessness could there be? What do you call a flaw? What are mind and eye? Could they be alike?

Thus the boy "lost" the mirror—is this not the boy dropping his skin and flesh? Yet even if your view is like this, so you understand that mind and eye are not separated and both people can see, actually this is a dualistic view. It is not one that has really clarified the self.

So do not entertain the view of a sphere, and do not conceive of the form of a body. You should investigate most meticulously, break through the objective and subjective at once, and realize that even your self is incomprehensible. Unless you reach this realm you are just beings formed by the results of your actions and do not yet comprehend the potential of buddhahood. In this way did Jayashata finally repent and leave home; becoming initiated, he subsequently spent years in attendance on Sanghanandi.

Once, hearing the sound of wind in the chimes in the hall, Sanghanandi asked Jayashata, "Is it the chimes ringing or the wind ringing?" This story should be examined thoroughly. Though Sanghanandi ultimately didn't see the chimes or the wind, still he asked this question to have Jayashata know what is what. What is this? You cannot understand in terms of wind and chimes—it is not ordinary wind chimes.

When the wind blew on the chimes, there was this koan; and Jayashata answered, "It is not the wind, not the chimes—it is just my mind ringing." Clearly there is no setting forth of any bounds of even a single atom. Thus "it is not the wind ringing or the chimes ringing—and if you think of it as ringing, then it is ringing." But such a view is still not the silence of the mind as well. Therefore he said, "My mind is ringing."

Hearing this story, people misunderstand and think it is not necessarily the wind's ringing—that "it is just mind ringing" and that this is supposedly why Jayashata spoke this way. In the naturally real spontaneous state when all things do not appear, how can you even say that it is not the ringing of chimes? Therefore "my mind is ringing."

There is a long distance in time between Jayashata and the sixth Zen patriarch of China, yet they are not separated: the sixth patriarch said, "The wind and flag are not moving—your minds are moving."

Now when you too penetrate through this mind ground, then past, present, and future are originally not separated. Realization is continuous past and present, so what difference can you discern? Don't discriminate with your ordinary views—you can only know it by its not being the ringing of the wind or the ringing of the chimes. If you want to know what it is, you must know it is your own mind ringing. The form of that ringing is like the soaring height of the mountains, like the plunging depths of the oceans. Even the profusion of plants and trees, and the lights of people's eyes, are the form of mind ringing.

So you shouldn't think of it as the ringing of a sound—sound too is the ringing of mind. The physical elements and mental clusters and all things are all as a whole the ringing of mind. There is never a time when this mind is not ringing; therefore after all it does not carry an echo. Also it is not heard by the ears; because ears *are* ringing, Jayashata said that all is silent.

When you see in this way, there is no place at all for myriad things to appear. Thus there are no forms of mountains, no forms of oceans—there is no longer a single thing with any shape or form. It is like riding a little boat on the ocean in a dream; whether you hoist sail and plow through the waves, or whether you stop the boat to determine the direction of the currents, there is no sky to float in, no bottom to sink to—what more mountains and seas are there that can be established outside? And what self is there sporting in the boat?

That is why Sanghanandi taught in this way: though there are eyes, they have no hearing; though there are ears, they have no vision. Therefore you should not say that the senses merge—there are no senses to be equipped with. That is why "all is silent." When you try to grasp them, there are no senses; when you try to abandon them, there are no sense fields. Senses and objects both shed, mind and environment are both forgotten. When you look closely, there are no senses or objects to shed, no mind or environment to obliterate. Truly peaceful and silent, it is not a question of sameness or difference, not a feeling of inside or outside.

When you truly reach such a state, then you receive and hold the treasure of the teaching of the Buddhas and rank among the Zen masters. If not, then even if you understand that all things are not mistaken, you are still maintaining your self and talking of others, and ultimately things are separate from each other. If they are separate, how can you commune with the Buddhas? It is like building boundary fences in the sky—how could the sky be blocked? It is just that you are creating obstructing boundaries yourself. Once the boundaries are broken, what would be considered inside or outside?

At this point, even Shakyamuni Buddha is not the beginning, you are not the end. There is no visage of the Buddhas at all, and no form of people either. When it is like this, just like clear water making waves, the Buddhas and Zen masters go on appearing—this is not increase and not decrease, yet the water flows and the waves go on peaking. Therefore you should actually reach such a realm by investigating thoroughly.

Since beginningless time and forever into the future, though we are temporarily creating divisions and arranging time frames of past, present, and future, yet from eon to eon it is all just like so. To comprehend this pure clear original nature, you cannot toil over it with skin and flesh, you cannot discern it by means of the movement or stillness of your body. This realm is not knowable at all by body-mind, not discernible by motion or stillness. It can only be attained by carefully making a penetrating investigation and stopping your own folly and realizing the truth by yourself.

If you do not understand in this way, you will be uselessly carrying your body and mind twenty-four hours a day, like carrying a heavy burden on your shoulders. After all body and mind won't rest easy. If you cast off body and mind, with the mind ground empty and open, you will attain to utmost normalcy.

But even if you are thus, as long as you cannot express and illumine the ringing of mind in the foregoing story, you do not know the appearance of the Buddhas and do not know the enlightenment of sentient beings. Therefore I want to add a humble saying to express the ringing of the mind:

The silent mind ringing echoes in ten thousand ways;
Sanghanandi, Jayashata, as well as the wind and chimes.

20

Kumarata

The Buddhist master Jayashata said to Kumarata, "In ancient times the Buddha predicted that a thousand years after his death a great man from Yuezhi would succeed to the mystic teaching and spread it. Now you have met me in fulfillment of this auspicious prophecy."

When Kumarata heard this, his knowledge of former lives was awakened.

Kumarata was from a priestly family of the Central Asian country of Yuezhi, north of India. In the past he had been a god in the heaven of freedom; there he saw a bodhisattva's ornaments and suddenly conceived love. Falling, he was born in the heaven of the thirty-three celestial mansions. There he heard the king of those gods speaking about transcendental wisdom, and because of the excellence of the teaching he ascended to the heaven of pure intellect, and because his faculties were sharp he skillfully expounded the essence of the teaching. The gods revered him as their guide, and when it came time for him to succeed to spiritual leadership in Buddhism he finally descended to Yuezhi.

The Buddhist master Jayashata went to Yuezhi on his teaching travels. Seeing an unusual atmosphere around one of the houses of the people of the priestly caste, he went to enter that house. Kumarata said, "What group is this?" Jayashata said, "In ancient times the Buddha predicted that a man from Yuezhi would inherit and propagate his teaching a thousand years after his death." It was then that Kumarata became aware of his past lives.

This story should be treated very carefully. Even if you clearly understand that the verbal teaching itself is a manifestation of buddha nature, or understand that birth and death, coming and going, is the true human body, if you do not realize that your own fundamental nature is empty and luminous, spiritual and spacious, you do not know the experience of the Buddhas.

Therefore you would be startled on seeing the light emanated by a bodhisattva, and upon seeing the marks and refinements of the Buddhas you would admire them. Why? Because you have not yet escaped the three poisons of greed, hatred, and folly.

Let us consider Kumarata's past causes. By love he regressed and fell and descended to a lower heaven, but due to past causes he happened to hear the king of the gods there expounding the teaching, and thereby ascended to a higher heaven. Later he came down to be born in Yuezhi. The virtues he had accumulated over the eons were not in vain; finally he met a master of Buddhism and realized knowledge of his former lives.

So-called knowledge of former lives is usually thought to mean knowing the past and future. What is the use of that? If you just observe that the original unchanging inherent nature has no holiness or profanity and no delusion, a hundred thousand teachings and innumerable wonderful meanings are all in the mind source.

Therefore the errors of sentient beings and the enlightenment of the Buddhas are both within one's own heart. It is not a phenomenon of sense, faculties, or sense data at all; it is not the form of mind or environment. When you reach this point, what can you consider past, what present? Which are the Buddhas, which sentient beings? There is not a single thing blocking the eyes, not a single mote of dust touching the hands.

There is just a mass of empty brightness, open and free, without bounds. The true Buddha whose realization of thusness has been fulfilled for an immensely long time is precisely the undimmed original sentient being. When you awake in this way, it is not increased; and when you do not know it, it is not decreased. Contacting the awareness that it has been *thus* since time immemorial is called the awakening of the knowledge of past lives.

Unless you reach this realm, you will uselessly be confused by feelings of delusion and enlightenment, be moved by appearances of coming and going, and ultimately fail to realize there is your own self. You will fail to realize that the original mind is not in error, by your failure causing Buddhas to take the trouble to appear in the world and making Zen masters come from far-off lands.

The original purpose of Buddhas appearing in the world and Zen masters communicating the teaching was just for this matter, not for anything else. You should concentrate closely and know it is spiritual, unclouded, radiant and bright, not concealed. Knowing that there is an original light is called knowledge of past lives.

Again I have a humble saying to convey a bit of the principle:

Pushing over the body of past lives blocked by experience,
Now he meets the same old fellow.

21

Jayata

Kumarata said to Jayata, "Although you believe in three kinds of karma, you do not yet understand that karma comes from confusion. Confusion is based on consciousness, consciousness depends on ignorance, ignorance depends on the mind. The mind is originally pure, having no origination or destruction; in it there is no fabrication, no retribution, no victory or defeat. It is serene and spiritual. If you penetrate this teaching, you can be the same as the Buddhas. All good and evil, contrived and uncontrived, are like dreams or illusions."

Jayata understood the message and realized knowledge of the past.

Jayata was from northern India. He was a man of profound knowledge and guided countless people. When he first met the Buddhist master Kumarata, he asked, "My parents have always been pious Buddhists, but they have been plagued by sickness and failure of their undertakings. Our neighbors, on the other hand, are butchers, yet they are always healthy and successful. What is their luck, and what is wrong with us?"

The Buddhist master said, "This is not hard to understand. There are three time frames in the consequences of good and evil. Whenever people see the good die young and the violent live long, or see the evil being lucky and the just suffering tragedy, they do not understand the past or future and are just deluded by the present situation. Therefore they think that there is no causality and that evil and virtue are naught. This is very stupid and foolish—they are like this because of ignorance in study of the Way."

The three kinds of karma are karma followed in the present, karma experienced in the next life, and karma followed later. Karma followed in the present means actions done in the present life whose effects are experienced in the same lifetime. Karma experienced in the next life means actions done in the present life whose effects are felt in the next life. Karma followed later means actions done in the present life whose effects come in later lifetimes, even in the distant future.

Therefore people may experience good in the present because of good deeds done in the past, yet it may be that present results are not the same because of past actions. Those who have purely good or purely bad active causes experience purely good or bad results of action in the present life. Those of mixed good and bad action experience mixed good and bad results.

Moreover, the power of cultivation of Buddhism changes grave karma so that it is experienced lightly, and changes light karma so that it no longer exists in the present. Evil causes in past ages should bring on grave suffering in the future, but it can happen that it is lightly experienced because of the power of Buddhist cultivation in this life. One may be plagued by disease, or nothing may turn out as one wishes, or else whatever one says may be slighted by others— these are all examples of lightly experiencing in this life the grave sufferings of the future.

So we should resort all the more to the power of Buddhist cultivation. The retributions prepared in the remote past can all be made light simply by vigorous effort. Although you have some understanding of the Way through your Zen study, you may get a bad name, or your undertakings may not work out as you want, and you may not be physically healthy either. If that is the case, think that it is transformation of the grave into relatively light experience; so even if people despise you, don't resent it, and even if people slander you, don't blame them. Though you might even pay respect and honor to these slanderers, what you should not do is hate them. Your work on the Way will grow daily, while your residual karma will vanish hourly. So you should study and practice carefully.

"Though you now believe in the three kinds of karma, you don't know the root of karma yet." Good and bad rewards of karma—action—are distinguished; ordinary and holy are different. All worlds, all states of being, all states of mind, are all results of karma. This karma arises from confusion. This confusion is hating and loving where we should not hate or love, judging right and wrong where right and wrong are not to be judged. Illusion is knowing as man what is not man, knowing as woman what is not woman, separating self and others. Ignorance is not knowing the root source of oneself and not knowing where myriad things are born. Lacking wisdom in all respects, losing wisdom in all places, is called nonenlightenment.

Without thought, without objects, this mind is originally pure and clear, not turning away to extraneous objects. Changing this mind is called ignorance. When you are aware of this ignorance, your own mind is originally pure and clear; it is spiritually illumined of its own nature.

When you can understand in this way, ignorance breaks up, the wheel of routine is empty, the various kinds of life in mundane existences quickly vanish. Everyone's original mind is like this. Thus there is no separation or barrier caused by birth and death, there are no created things. Thus there is no hatred, no love, no increase, no decrease—only silent peace, sublime awareness.

If you want to see your original basic mind, put down myriad concerns, set all mental involvements to rest; don't think of good or bad, and for now set your eyes on the tip of your nose and look at your original mind. When the one mind is silent, all forms done with, then the branches and leaves—karma and its results—do not remain.

So you do not stay in the realm of nondiscrimination, you are not confined to the sphere of inconceivability. It is not permanent, not impermanent; it is not that the original mind has ignorance, nor is it that it is pure. There is no separation of the Buddhas, no distinction of sentient beings. When you arrive at the realm of pure clear complete illumination, for the first time you will be the same as Buddha.

When you reach here, everything conditioned and unconditioned is all ended and is like a dream, an illusion. Though you try to grasp, your hand is empty; though you try to see, nothing catches the eye.

When you have arrived at this realm, you understand the essence before the Buddhas appeared in the world, you get to where sentient beings have not yet erred. Unless your study has reached this state, even if you prostrate yourself before a statue of Buddha all day and tune your mind and body during your daily activities, this is just leading to higher states of mind, with contaminated reward still remaining. It is like the shadow following the form; though it exists, it is not real. Therefore you should concentrate your energies and clarify your original mind.

As usual I add a humble saying:

The camphor tree, as ever, grows to the sky;
The branches and leaves, roots and trunk, flourish beyond the
    clouds.

22

Vasubandhu

Jayata said, "I do not seek the Way, yet I am not confused. I do not pay obeisance to Buddha, yet I do not disregard Buddha either. I do not sit for long periods, yet I am not lazy. I do not limit my meals, yet I do not eat indiscriminately either. I am not contented, yet I am not greedy. When the mind does not seek anything, this is called the Way."

When Vasubandhu heard this, he discovered uncontaminated knowledge.

Vasubandhu became a Buddhist monk when he was fifteen years old, and subsequently he became a leading debater. Eventually the Buddhist master Jayata came to Vasubandhu's area on a teaching journey, expounding the doctrine of sudden realization. There he found a group of students of philosophy whose chief was Vasubandhu.

This Vasubandhu always limited his meals to one a day, never lay down to sleep, and performed ritual obeisances to an image of Buddha six times a day. He was pure and desireless, regarded as an ideal by the group.

Jayata wanted to liberate Vasubandhu, so he first asked the group, "This ascetic Vasubandhu practices pure conduct well, but can he attain the Buddha Way?" The group said, "Our teacher is very diligent—how could there be anything wrong with him?" Jayata said,

"Your teacher is far from the Way. Even if one practices asceticism for eons, it is all the root of illusion." The group said, "What virtue do you have, that you criticize our teacher?" Jayata said, "I don't seek enlightenment, yet I am not confused," and so on, as in the opening story. Finally Vasubandhu realized uncontaminated knowledge, whereupon he joyfully praised the Buddhist master Jayata.

Jayata also said to that group, "Do you understand my words? My reason for saying what I did is that his search for enlightenment was too eager. If the harp string is too tight it will snap. Therefore I did not praise him, but made him abide in the state of peace and enter the knowledge of all Buddhas."

In this story in particular we find the most essential secret of study of the Way. If you think there is buddhahood to attain and a Way to find, and if you fast or do ascetic exercises with that thought, or sit for long periods of time without lying down, or do prostrations and recite scriptures, trying to build up merits for attaining the Way, all of this is raining flowers in the flowerless sky, making holes where there are no holes. Even if you pass eons in this way, you will never have a bit of liberation. Indeed, not craving anything is called the Way, so even if it is contentment you want, this is still based on greed.

If you must indulge in sitting for a long time, this is the error of attachment to the body. If you would eat only once a day, this is still seeing food. And if you would do prostrations and recite scriptures, this is making flowers in the eyes. Therefore every one of these practices is based on illusion; it is not your original self.

The disciples of Buddha set up various kinds of pure regulations to show the disciplined behavior of Buddhas and Zen masters. Clinging to them obsessively becomes an affliction, however, a passion. Furthermore, if you must reject birth and death to seek the Way beyond, yet you cannot cut off the beginningless process of dying in one place and being born in another—what state would you consider attainment of the Way? Yet you want to seek the Way while still caught up in all these things—it is all a misunderstanding.

What further buddhahood to attain do you see? What sentient beings do you see who can be deluded? There is no one who is deluded, no doctrine to realize. For this reason, though we speak of overturning delusion to attain enlightenment, or of transforming ordinary people into sages, all this is talk for people who are not yet enlightened. What ordinariness is there to transform? What delusion is there to awaken from? This is why Zen master Jiashan said, "Clearly there is no phenomenon of enlightenment; the doctrine of enlightenment deludes people. Stretch out your legs and sleep—there is no falsehood and no reality." The essence of the Way is truly like this.

Yet even though this be so, beginners should study carefully to actually arrive at this stage of equanimity and peace. For if you yourself have no genuine understanding, you may be deluded by the words of others. So if you try to lift your eyes to see, you will be invaded by the buddha demon. Today even though you hear such talk and understand that there is nothing to attain, yet if a teacher tells you there is some doctrine to realize, or if a buddha demon comes and tells you there is some method to practice, ultimately your mind will be stirred and you will go astray.

Now, accepting the true teaching of all Buddhas and investigating it carefully and thoroughly, you should reach the realm where you are yourself at peace. Someone who has attained peace is like someone who has had enough to eat—even a regal feast would no longer be appealing. This is why it is said that fine food is not for the satisfied to eat. An ancient said, "Once troubled, finally at rest."

When you look carefully, your own original mind does not see Buddha, does not see sentient beings—how could there be any delusion to reject or any enlightenment to seek? Ever since the Zen founder came from India to get people to see directly, Zen teachers have had people sit up single-mindedly and rest peacefully in themselves, without question of their learning or experience.

You have thought mistaken what has never been mistaken. Do not waste time just concerning yourself with the frost on other people's yards and forget about the treasure in your own house.

So now you have met a close friend. Do not hope for enlightenment on another day far in the future. Just look within your own heart, examining carefully—do not seek from another. If you can do this, hundreds of thousands of teachings and boundless buddha works all flow from here, covering the heavens and the earth. Just don't seek the Way—all you need to do is maintain your true self.

If you do not know of the existence of your true self even though it has always been with you, you are like someone holding something in his hands while at the same time looking here and there for that very thing. What a mistake this is! This is just forgetting one's true self.

Now as we look at the matter closely, the sublime path of the Buddhas and the pure tradition of the Zen masters too are in this one thing alone. You should not doubt this. When you reach this stage you will not doubt what the Zen masters say.

In the foregoing story it says that when Vasubandhu heard this he realized uncontaminated knowledge. If you want to realize uncontaminated knowledge, you should maintain your true self. If you want to maintain your true self, you should know that from birth to death it is just *this*. There is not a single mote of dust to reject, not a single doctrine to grasp. And don't particularly think of realizing uncontaminated knowledge either.

As usual, I have a humble saying to explain the story:

The wind traverses the vast sky,
clouds emerge from the mountains;
Feelings of enlightenment and things of the world
are of no concern at all.

23

Manora

Manora asked Vasubandhu, "What is the enlightenment of the Buddhas?" Vasubandhu said, "It is the original nature of the mind." Manora then asked, "What is the original nature of the mind?" Vasubandhu said, "It is the emptiness of the elements of sense faculties, sense consciousnesses, and sense data."

Manora was enlightened on hearing this.

Manora was a son of the rajah of the kingdom of Nadi. He met Vasubandhu when he was thirty years old, when Vasubandhu came to Nadi in the course of his travels. The rajah asked Vasubandhu, "Why are the customs of Rajagrha (Vasubandhu's homeland) different from here?" Vasubandhu said, "In that land three Buddhas have appeared in the world. Now in your kingdom there are two teachers of the Way." The rajah said, "Who are these two teachers?" Vasubandhu said, "The Buddha predicted that in the second five hundred years after his death there would be a great man with spiritual power who would leave home and succeed to the saints. Your second son Manora is just such a man. And though my virtue is slight, I am the other teacher." The rajah said, "If it is as you say, I should give up my son and make him a mendicant." Vasubandhu said, "Very good, your majesty, you are following the Buddha's message well." So he then transmitted the precepts to Manora.

After that Manora attended Vasubandhu. At one point he asked,

"What is the enlightenment of the Buddhas?" Vasubandhu said, "It is the original nature of the mind." This is precisely what should be asked in the beginning of the study of the Way. Enlightenment means the Way. Therefore this question means "What is the Way?" People these days do not ask about the teaching with an open mind, and do not study with teachers as beginners, so they don't ask this question. If you have a genuine aspiration for enlightenment, you shouldn't be this way. First you should ask what Buddha is, then you should ask what the Way of buddhahood is. That is why Manora asked this question. And Vasubandhu answered, "It is the original nature of the mind." Now because he was single-minded and didn't cling to anything, Manora then asked what the original nature of mind is. Vasubandhu answered that it is the emptiness of the elements of sense—faculties, consciousness, and data. Manora was then enlightened.

Buddha is none other than the basic nature of the mind. This original nature is ultimately unknowable and imperceptible, indeed the unexcelled Way. So the mind has no form and no abode. Of course "Buddha" and "the Way" are both forced names. Therefore Buddha is not conscious knowledge, the Way is not something cultivated. Mind is not conscious knowledge either. This realm has no objects and no faculties—where can consciousness be established? This is why he said that all these elements being empty is the original nature of mind.

So do not talk about this state in terms of mind and objects, do not understand it as cognitive knowledge. At this point the Buddhas ultimately do not appear, and the ineffable Way also does not need cultivation or maintenance. Furthermore, though perception and awareness may have no traces, sound, form, and motion cannot have boundaries. Therefore it is said, "This is identical to seeing and hearing, yet is not seeing and hearing; there is no more sound and color to present to you. If you understand that there is nothing here at all, what does it matter if substance and function be distinguished or not?"

Thus you should not understand "sound" here in terms of tone and pitch, and you should not understand "color" here in terms of blue, yellow, red, or white. Don't consider sight the correspondent of the light of the eyes, don't think hearing is the faculty of the ears. No one has eyes or ears as partners to color and sound. If you say there is correspondence between the ear and sound, or that the eye relates to form and color, you don't understand sound, you are ignorant about eyes.

For if you say there is something related to, then how does sound enter the ear, how can form be seen in the eye? Therefore, unless it is like space merging with space, like water mixing with water, hearing and seeing are impossible, for otherwise a sound would always remain in the ear and a form would always remain in the eye. Because this is not so, the eye communes with forms and colors, the ear with sounds, merging without separation, fusing without tracks.

This being so, even a sound that can make heaven and earth reverberate enters a tiny ear—isn't this a case of "the largest is the same as small"? And with a tiny eye you can see the whole world—isn't this "the smallest is the same as the large"? Is it not that the eye is form and color, and sound is the ear? Knowing this, you understand in this way. This mind has no borders, no boundaries, no sides or surfaces. Therefore the eye basically does not apprehend anything, forms and colors cannot divide. Is it not that faculties, consciousnesses, and data of sense are all empty?

Therefore when you reach this realm, you can say it is sound, you can say it is the eye, you can say it is consciousness. "Thus" is all right, "not thus" is all right too—"thus" and "not thus" are both all right. Nothing comes from outside, there is no boundary, nothing separating. Therefore when you speak in terms of sound, both hearing and speaking are discerned in sound; when you speak in terms of form and color, both subject and object are set within form and color—there is nothing outside.

But you people don't understand this principle. You may think that sound and form are false and should be erased, that the original mind is fundamentally permanent and cannot change or move. This is laughable. In this realm, what thing can change or not change? What can be real or not real?

So if you do not clearly understand this matter, you will not understand either the fields of perception or perception itself, and will therefore try not to see or hear. This is tying yourself up without rope, falling where there is no hole. Because of this you cannot escape defilement by feelings and leaking of your mental energy.

If you investigate thoroughly, and if you penetrate the depths and see clearly, you will rise unhindered to the very heights.

Again I have a humble saying to illustrate this story:

The spirit of emptiness is not inside or outside;
Seeing, hearing, sound and form, all are void.

24

Haklena

The Buddhist master Manora said to Haklena, "I have the treasure of the unexcelled great teaching; you should listen to it, accept it, and teach in the future."

Hearing this, Haklena attained enlightenment.

Haklena, from the country of Yuezhi, was from a family of the priestly caste. His parents had been without issue until they prayed at a Buddhist shrine; that night his mother dreamed that a spiritual boy from atop the polar mountain, bearing a gold ring, announced his arrival, and on awakening she found she was pregnant.

When he was seven years old, Haklena saw the village people performing superstitious sacrifices. He went into the shrine and upbraided the spirit of the shrine, saying, "You are deluding people, arbitrarily creating calamity and fortune. Every year you waste cattle and sheep for sacrifices, cruelly having them killed." When he had said this, the shrine suddenly collapsed. Because of this the villagers called him a holy child. When he was twenty-two he became a Buddhist monk, and when he was thirty he met the Buddhist master Manora.

When he first met Manora, there were various extraordinary occurrences. I should mention them all, but I'll just bring up one story. Haklena said to master Manora, "What is the reason I am followed by a group of cranes?" For Haklena was always accompanied by a flock of cranes.

Manora said, "You were once a monk in the fourth eon. As you were going to a meeting in the dragon palace, your disciples wanted to go along with you, but you saw no one among your five hundred disciples worthy of the sublime offerings of the dragons. At that time your disciples said to you, 'You always preach that what is equal in respect to food is equal in respect to all things. What is the wisdom in your refusal to act in accord with this now?' So you let them go. Although you were reborn in various different countries after you died, your five hundred disciples, because of their lack of virtue, were born among feathered beings. Now, feeling your benevolence, they have become cranes and follow you."

When Haklena heard this, he asked, "By what means shall I liberate them?" Manora said, "I have the unexcelled treasure of the true teaching."

In truth, the principle of equality of food and equality of all things draws no distinction between sages and ordinary people. But as a matter of principle, though both teacher and students went to the dragon palace, because those with slight merit and virtue were not worthy of the sublime offerings there, they became birds. This story should be a warning to students.

Now there is no discrimination in teaching the true nature of things, and food also should be equal. Yet there are those who can digest the donations of the faithful, and there are those who are harmed by the donations of the faithful. At this point it would seem as if they were not equal, that we should say there is discrimination. The reason for this is that if you see "food" and see "the teaching," though you may see that they are equal and understand that they are the same for all, you are still seeing food and seeing a teaching and haven't escaped a dualistic view. Deluded by covetousness, those disciples followed their teacher, and as a result eventually became birds. So we know that they hadn't arrived at the principle of equality in food and equality in truth. Indeed, they were bound by forms and appearances.

The supreme teaching referred to has nothing of food or of doctrine or of things. What is sacred, what is profane? It is not something that can be reached by form or shadow. It can hardly even be called mind or nature. This "teaching" is not received from Buddhas or

Zen masters, it is not given to one's children, not inherited from one's parents. It has nothing that can be called self or other. Where can the names of food or phenomena come from? Is there any place to answer an invitation? Is there any turning into birds?

So you must look closely, meditate thoroughly, and first know that the original nature of your own mind is an open awareness, wondrously clear and bright. Be able to maintain it and thoroughly mature it, and then know that there is also the phenomenon of the Buddhas' transmission of the lamp of enlightenment.

Even if you have understood the essence of the original nature of your own mind and are as liberated as the Buddhas and Zen masters, there is still a supreme treasury of truth that can illumine the future. This is not the principle of the original nature, much less an object of perception. It far transcends ideas of antiquity and modernity, and has never remained in the realm of sentient beings or Buddhas. Therefore such a person cannot even be called a Buddha, nor can such a person be considered ordinary. Such people neither sit in the hall upright nor tend to either side; so not even their shadows can be found, nor can their tracks be discovered.

If you have reached this state, what is "the nature of the mind"? What is "enlightenment"? Spit it all out at once, shit it all out at once. When you can do so, you are a person beyond measure. If you do not reach such a state, you are still an ordinary mortal.

So you should see closely and aspire to bear the supreme treasure of the great teaching. Then the body of Buddha will still be alive. Just don't cling to names and worry about forms. In Zen study you must discern reality.

I have a humble saying to illustrate this principle:

A powdered wall sticking through the clouds—
snow on the massive crags.
Absolute purity without a blotch
is different from the blue sky.

25

Sinha

Sinha asked the Buddhist master Haklena, "I want to seek enlightenment—how should I apply my mind?" Haklena said, "If you seek enlightenment, there is no way to apply the mind to it." Sinha said, "If there's no way to apply the mind, who does the work of Buddhas?" Haklena said, "If you apply anything, this is not virtue; if you don't contrive anything, this is the work of Buddhas. A scripture says, 'The virtues I practice are not mine.'"

Hearing this, Sinha gained access to the wisdom of Buddhas.

Sinha was from central India, born to a family of the priestly caste. Originally he was a Hindu scholar, but later he called on the Buddhist master Haklena and directly encountered the state where there is nowhere to apply the mind, thus entering suddenly in the wisdom of Buddhas.

Now Haklena pointed to the northwest and said, "What is that atmospheric sign?" Sinha said, "It looks to me like a white rainbow extending from the sky to the earth, crossed by five black vapors." Haklena said, "What does it portend?" Sinha said, "I have no idea." Haklena said, "Fifty years after my death there will be trouble in northern India, and it will affect you. Even so, you should transmit my spiritual teaching for the education of the future."

Having received this secret prediction, Sinha went to teach in Kashmir. There he found Vashashita, who was to become his spiritual heir. He told Vashashita about Haklena's prediction, and sent him to take the Way to another land and teach there.

Now at this time the king of Kashmir was deeply devoted to Buddhism, but he was still fascinated by appearances. As it happened, there were two magicians in that country who tried to stir up trouble. Assuming the appearance of Buddhist monks, they stole into the royal palace with the intention of blaming their actions on the Buddhists if they were apprehended.

The two magicians were in fact arrested, and the king did blame the Buddhists. Outraged, he had monasteries destroyed and the Buddhist monks and nuns driven out. He also personally took a sword and went to the Buddhist master Sinha. He asked Sinha, "Have you attained emptiness of body and mind?" Sinha said, "Yes." The king said, "Are you detached from birth and death?" Sinha said, "Yes." The king said, "If so, give me your head." Sinha said, "This body is not my own possession—why should I begrudge the head?"

The king then swung the sword and cut off Sinha's head. White milk gushed from the neck up to a height of several dozen yards, and the king's right arm fell off. After seven days the king died.

That was the end of master Sinha.

When teacher and apprentice first met, Sinha asked the Buddhist master Haklena, "I want to seek enlightenment—how should I apply my mind?" Haklena said, "If you seek enlightenment, there's nothing to apply the mind to." When one really and truly seeks enlightenment, how could it have anything to do with using the mind? Here we die, there we are born. Though we aspire to enlightenment and seek truth here and there, the fact that now we have not arrived at the ultimate reality is basically because of using this mind.

So if you want to accord instantly with enlightened wisdom, it is not only a matter of detaching from false views and mental poisons; you must also detach from the bodies and knowledges of Buddhas. When you practice in this way, you cannot be relegated to the state of the ordinary person or exalted to the rank of a Buddha. You transcend far beyond the realm of the sense of holy or ordinary, and leave behind assessment of difference and sameness.

Therefore it is said that even Buddhas and Zen masters can hardly reach the realm of mysterious wonder. It is not just that Buddhas and Zen masters cannot reach it—basically, when you talk about this realm, ultimately Buddhas and Zen masters do not even exist. Reaching such a realm is called the true essence of seeking enlightenment.

If you are not yet thus, even if you can make flowers shower and cause the earth to move, expounding the nature of mind and discoursing on esoteric marvels, you have not even glimpsed the true ineffable Way. So you should experientially arrive at this mysterious realm and clarify that which all the Zen masters bore.

To explain a little bit of principle, as usual I have a humble saying:

If you want to reveal the void, do not cover it up;
Thoroughly empty, pure and peaceful, it is originally clear.

26

Vashashita

The Buddhist master Sinha said to Vashashita, "I now hand over to you the treasury of the eye of the true teaching of Buddha; you should guard it for the universal benefit of the future."

Sinha discovered the preexistent basis and personally inherited the mind seal.

Vashashita was from Kashmir, born to a family of the priestly caste. His mother dreamed she had gotten a magical sword, and found she was pregnant.

When the Buddhist master Sinha came to Kashmir on his teaching travels, there were five groups of seekers there: those who practiced meditation, those who cultivated knowledge, those who clung to forms, those who rejected forms, and those who did not speak. Sinha unified these groups, and his fame spread far and near.

When Sinha was looking for a successor, he met a householder who brought his son to the Buddhist master and said, "This boy's name is Shita. When he was born, his left hand was closed in a fist, and though he is now grown he still cannot open his hand. Please tell us the underlying cause."

Sinha looked at the youth, took him by the hand, and said, "Give me back the jewel." The youth immediately opened his hand and gave him a jewel. Everyone was amazed. Sinha said, "In a past life I was a monk and had a boy attendant named Vasha. I went to a feast on the western seaboard once and received a jewel as a gift. I entrusted the jewel to the boy, so it is reasonable that he now return it to me." The man then gave up his son and allowed him to leave home and become a mendicant. The Buddhist master then ordained him and invested him with the precepts. Because of the boy's past condition he named him Vashashita.

Finally, in making his bequest to Vashashita, Sinha said to him, "I now hand over to you the treasury of the eye of the true teaching of the Buddha; you should guard it well and pass it on to the future." Vashashita's discovery of his former condition refers to his having been the boy Vasha in a past life, entrusted with a jewel by the Buddhist master; now, having entered a womb and having been born in another family, he still kept the jewel, and finally presented it to master Sinha.

By this we should know that this causal nexus should not necessarily be said to be the sole existence of a real body after the disintegration of the flesh body. If this body is a perishable body, how could he now still be holding the jewel? Thus we should know that relinquishing life and being reborn is not a matter of physical death.

At this point we should not say that the physical body disintegrates and one thing remains forever as the eternal spirit. What sort of thing would the eternal spirit be? It is only a matter of the appearance of the relinquishment of the body and the appearance of incarnation, that is all.

Therefore we must say that before and after are not two, past and present are not different. Thus this should not be called body, nor should it be called mind. Since it is not divided into mind and body, we should not divide it into past and present. Therefore it is *thus*.

It is not only Vasha who is thus; in reality, everyone is thus. Hence there is no place of birth, nor of death; it is just a matter of changing heads and faces with time. It is not necessarily a change and renewal of the physical body and psychophysical clusters. There has never been any covering by a mass of flesh or supporting by bones. Even if there are thousands of forms and types, all are the original mind light. It is because of not knowing this that we think this one is young and that one is old. There is no substance of old age, and originally no youth. So how can we divide birth and death and distinguish before and after?

Therefore, pointing out that Vasha of a former age and Shita of the present are not two bodies is the preexistent basis. Thus he transmitted the treasury of the eye of the true teaching of the Buddha to benefit the future.

So we should know that the Buddhas and Zen masters fundamentally have never been enlightened, ignorant people ultimately are not lost. Sometimes they cultivate spiritual practices, sometimes they awaken the will for enlightenment; enlightenment and awakening the will basically have no end or beginning. Sentient beings and Buddhas are originally not inferior or superior. It is just *thusness* everywhere.

Therefore it is simply a matter of always maintaining the trust in this way and not forgetting the preexistent basis.

To explain this story, as usual I have a humble saying:

Blooming flowers, falling leaves, when they directly show,
The medicine tree fundamentally has no different flavor.

27

Punyamitra

When Punyamitra was a prince, the Buddhist master Vashashita asked him, "Why do you want to leave home?" Punyamitra said, "If I leave home, it is not for anything else." Vashashita said, "Not for what?" Punyamitra said, "Not for anything mundane." Vashashita said, "Then for what?" Punyamitra said, "To do buddha work." Vashashita said, "Your wisdom is natural; you must be an incarnation of one of the sages." Then the Buddhist master permitted the prince Punyamitra to leave home and become a mendicant.

Punyamitra was the crown prince of a kingdom in southern India. The Buddhist master Vashashita came to southern India after converting the Hindu Anatmanatha in central India. The king of that south Indian kingdom was called Devaguna; he welcomed the Buddhist master Vashashita and made offerings to him. The king had two sons, one of whom was violent and powerful, the other gentle and sickly. The Buddhist master expounded causality to them, and the king was suddenly relieved of doubt.

After that king died, his son, who was Punyamitra's father, assumed the throne. He believed in Hinduism and caused trouble for the Buddhist master Vashashita. Punyamitra was imprisoned for coming forth and admonishing his father about bothering the Buddhist master. The king suddenly asked the master, "My country has always been free of the weird and the strange—what religion is it that you are disseminating?"

Vashashita said, "There has actually been no false teaching in your country since ancient times. What I transmit is the religion of Buddha."

The king said, "The Buddha has been dead for twelve hundred years; from whom did you get this teaching?" Vashashita said, "The great Kashyapa personally received the Buddha's seal, and it has continued for twenty-four generations to the venerable Sinha; I received it from him."

The king said, "I have heard that the monk Sinha was unable to avoid being executed; how could he transmit the teaching to a successor?" Vashashita said, "Before my teacher's persecution occurred he secretly handed on to me the robe of faith and a verse of the teaching indicating successorship."

The king said, "Where is the robe?" The Buddhist master brought it forth from his bag and showed it to the king. The king commanded that it be burned. Five colors blazed forth in the fire, but when the fuel was exhausted the robe remained as before. The king then repented and prostrated himself, realizing that this was the true successor of Sinha. Then he pardoned his son, who now wanted to leave home and become a mendicant. The Buddhist master Vashashita asked him, "Why do you want to leave home?" Finally he permitted Punyamitra to become a Buddhist monk.

After that Punyamitra attended Vashashita for six years. Finally transmitting the Buddha's treasury of the eye of the truth to him, Vashashita said, "From the Buddha it has been handed down from successor to successor, up to the present; now you must receive and hold it, to enlighten all beings." When Punyamitra received this private direction, he felt a physical and mental sense of relief.

The story shows that Punyamitra did not have any ulterior motive for becoming a monk. Vashashita asked him what he wanted to leave home for, and he said he wanted to do buddha work. From this we should know that mendicants basically do not do anything for mundane purposes. Buddha work is not for oneself, nor for others, so it is not for anything ordinary.

Even if you shave your head and don monastic robes, assuming the appearance of a Buddhist mendicant, this does not mean you have escaped ideas of self and other. If you are not detached from appearances of maleness and femaleness, whatever you do is mundane activity, not buddha work.

Although it is true that when we speak for the moment from the point of view of people's original mind, there is no buddha work and no mundane concerns, as long as you do not know the original mind, whatever you do is a mundane affair. Understanding the original mind is called buddha work.

When you actually know the original mind, there is not even any sign of birth or of death, much less delusion or enlightenment. When you see in this way, even the physical and psychological elements do not remain, much less their various states of being. So there is no home to abandon, no body to set aside—therefore this is called "leaving home."

Because there is nowhere to dwell, the home is broken up and the person is gone. Therefore samsara and nirvana both disappear without being effaced, enlightenment and affliction are originally irrelevant without being abandoned. It is not only like this now; from age to age, it is not changed by phases of becoming, subsistence, decay, and emptiness, it is not bound by appearances of birth, life, change, and death. Open as space without inside or outside, clear as pure water—such is the original mind that is in everyone. So you shouldn't fear home life, and shouldn't be proud of leaving home. Just stop seeking outwardly; turn to yourself to understand.

For the moment try this: do not scatter your mind, do not look around, but observe carefully—now what can you call self, what can you call other? Since there is no polarity of self and other, what do you call good or bad? If you can do this, the original mind is basically evident, as clearly as the sun and moon, illumining everywhere.

Again I have a humble saying to express this story:

The original ground is level, without a blade of grass—
Where can Zen teaching make an arrangement?

28

Prajnatara

The Buddhist master Punyamitra said to Prajnatara, "Do you remember events of the past?" Prajnatara said, "I remember in a distant eon I was living in the same place as you; you were expounding great wisdom and I was reciting the most profound scripture. This event today is in conformity with past cause."

Prajnatara was from eastern India. In his time Punyamitra came to eastern India, where there was a king known as The Resolute who was a Hindu worshiper, his guru a Brahmin ascetic with long nails. When the Buddhist master Punyamitra was about to arrive, the king and the ascetic both saw a white vapor extending from above to below. The king said, "What omen is this?" The ascetic already knew that the Buddhist master had entered the realm, and he was afraid that he would gain the king's favor, so he said, "This is just a sign of a demon coming. This is not an auspicious omen."

The ascetic gathered his followers together and said to them, "Punyamitra is about to enter the capital city; who can defeat him?" A disciple said, "We each have various magical spells by which we can even move the heavens and the earth, or even enter water and fire; what is there to worry about?"

When the Buddhist master Punyamitra arrived, he first saw a black atmosphere around the palace walls. He said, "This will be just a little difficulty," and went straight to the king. The king said,

"What did you come here for?" The Buddhist master said, "I came to liberate sentient beings." The king said, "By what method do you liberate them?" Punyamitra said, "I liberate each according to kind."

The Hindu ascetic heard these words and could not control his anger; he then magically produced a mountain on top of the Buddhist master's head. Punyamitra pointed at the magical mountain, and suddenly it was on the heads of the ascetic's followers. They were all terrified and submitted to the Buddhist master. Punyamitra pitied them for their ignorance and delusion, and pointed at the mountain again, whereupon it disappeared. Then he expounded the essentials of Buddhism to the king, inducing him to incline to true religion.

Punyamitra also said to the king, "In this country there is a sage who will succeed me." At that time there was a young man of the priestly caste, about twenty years old, who had been orphaned since childhood and did not know his family name. Some called him Keyura, so people referred to him by that name. He spent the days wandering through the villages begging. He was just like the Buddhist saint who never despised anyone. When people asked him why he was going so fast, he would answer, "Why are you going so slow?" If someone asked his family name, he would reply, "Same as yours." No one knew what he meant.

Later, the king and the Buddhist master Punyamitra went out together riding in a chariot. Seeing the youth Keyura bowing his head before them, the Buddhist master said to him, "Do you remember past events?" And so the story goes, their meeting being in accord with past cause. Punyamitra also said to the king, "This youth is none other than Mahasthamaprapta Bodhisattva. This sage will produce two enlightened disciples; one will teach in southern India, the other has affinity in China. After four or five years he will want to return here." Finally, because of the past cause, he named the youth Prajnatara, "Pearl of Wisdom."

Now the founding teachers who transmitted the seal of the enlightened mind, the sages whose mind ground was opened and illumined, were arhats or bodhisattvas—saints of the individual and collective Buddhist paths—yet because they were not ignorant of the fundamental Way they were eternally enlightened ones. Even if you seem to be a beginner, if in a single moment the mind is turned around to reveal its originally inherent qualities, nothing is lacking at all; together with the realized ones, you will commune with the Buddhas. Though it is not a matter of one appearing and one disappearing, it is not a matter of together putting forth a single hand; there is no multiplicity, no different lineage.

Therefore seeing today is seeing all time; looking over the ages is guarding the present. The enlightened ones are born together with you and live together with me, without the slightest separation, accompanying us at all times. When you manage to arrive at this state, it is not something of past, present, or future, it is not a matter of sense, objects, or sense consciousnesses. This is why it is said that succession to the reality of Buddhism transcends time, that realization continuously pervades time. Because it is so, the golden needle and jade thread pass through finely. When you look closely, which is other, which is self? Neither the frame nor the point shows. Here everyone gets a seat, and it is always shared.

Therefore in the foregoing story too it says, "You were expounding great wisdom and I was reciting the most profound scripture." If form is pure, then omniscience is pure. There is no difference, no distinction. Sentient beings are the buddha nature, the buddha nature is sentient beings. The teacher does not introduce anything from outside, the student does not bring out anything from inside. Though the two are distinguished in this way, ultimately there is no difference in plurality.

Therefore Prajnatara was named "Pearl of Wisdom" in the same way as the Buddhist master Vashashita was named in accord with past cause and present condition. Past and present cannot be separated. How can emptiness and existence be different? This is why an ancient said, "If you can understand here, there is no problem; what is wrong with distinguishing or not distinguishing substance and function?"

When we consider emptiness the substance of myriad forms, there is nothing before us; when we consider myriad forms the function of emptiness, there is no different road. Therefore at this point the path of teacher and apprentice is transmitted. Even to understand that the seal of approval of Buddhas and Zen masters is of many kinds seems to suggest that there are divisions; yet even if you understand that there is no duality, you are still carrying a one-sided view. When you examine and evaluate carefully, when a white heron stands in the snow they are not the same color, and white flowers and moonlight are not exactly like each other. Traveling in this way, you go on "filling a silver bowl with snow, hiding a heron in the moonlight."

To analyze the foregoing story, I have a humble saying:

The light of the moon reflected in the depths of the pond is
    bright in the sky;
The water flowing to the horizon is thoroughly clear and pure.
Sifting and straining over and over, even if you know it exists,
Boundless and clear, it turns out to be utterly ineffable.

29

Bodhidharma

The Buddhist master Prajnatara asked Bodhidharma, "What among things is formless?" Bodhidharma said, "Nonorigination is formless." Prajnatara asked, "What among things is greatest?" Bodhidharma said, "The nature of reality is greatest."

Bodhidharma was from a family of the warrior caste, and his original name was Bodhitara. He was the third son of a rajah, or king, of southern India. That king was unusually devoted to Buddhism, and he once gave a priceless jewel to the Buddhist master Prajnatara.

The king had three sons, one named Chandratara, the second named Gunatara, and the third named Bodhitara. In order to test the wisdom of the princes, Prajnatara showed the jewel given him by their father and said, "Is there anything comparable to this jewel?" The first and second princes said, "This jewel is the finest of precious stones; there is certainly none better. Who but someone of your sanctity could receive such a jewel?"

But the third son Bodhitara said, "This is a worldly jewel, and cannot be considered of the highest order. Among all jewels, the jewel of truth is supreme. This is a worldly luster, and cannot be considered the finest. Among all lusters, the luster of wisdom is supreme. This is a worldly clarity, and cannot be considered the best. Among all clarities, clarity of mind is supreme. The sparkle of this jewel cannot shine by itself, it needs the light of knowledge to discern its sparkle. When you discern this, you know it is a jewel; when you know this jewel, you know it is precious. When you understand that it is precious, the value is not value in itself. If you understand the jewel, the jewel is not a jewel in itself.

"The jewel is not a jewel in itself because we need the jewel of knowledge to distinguish it as a jewel in the worldly sense. Value is not value in itself because we need the treasure of knowledge to understand the value of truth. Because your Way is a treasure of knowledge, you have been rewarded with a worldly treasure. So that treasure has appeared because there is enlightenment in you, just as the treasure of mind appears in anyone with enlightenment."

Hearing the eloquent explanation of the third prince, the Buddhist master Prajnatara knew that he was an incarnated sage and perceived that the prince would be his spiritual successor. He knew the time was not yet ripe, however, so he kept silent and did not single him out.

Later Prajnatara asked the youngest prince, "What among all things is formless?" The prince said, "Nonorigination is formless." The Buddhist master asked, "What among things is paramount?" The prince said, "The sense of self and others is paramount." Finally Prajnatara asked, "What among things is greatest?" The prince said, "The nature of reality is greatest." Although the minds of teacher and apprentice communicated through such dialogue, Prajnatara still waited for the opportunity to ripen.

Subsequently, when the king died and everyone was mourning, Bodhitara sat alone in front of the casket and went into a trance. He came out of the trance seven days later, then went to Prajnatara to request ordination as a Buddhist monk.

Prajnatara knew the time had come, so he ordained the prince and invested him with the precepts. After that Bodhitara sat in meditation for seven days in Prajnatara's presence, and Prajnatara gave him thorough instructions in the subtle principles of meditation. Hearing these instructions, Bodhitara developed unsurpassed wisdom. Then Prajnatara said to him, "You have already attained full comprehension of all principles. Dharma has the meaning of greatness of comprehension, so you should be called Dharma." Thus he changed his name to Bodhidharma.

Having been initiated and having received the teaching, Bodhidharma knelt and asked, "I have already realized the truth—to what land shall I go to work?" Prajnatara instructed him, "Though you have realized the truth, you should stay in southern India for a while; sixty-seven years after my death, you should go to China and teach those of great potential."

Bodhidharma said, "Will I be able to find great people with the capacity for the teaching? Will trouble arise after a thousand years?" Prajnatara said, "Innumerable people in that land will attain enlightenment. There will be a little trouble. You should humble yourself. When you get to China, don't stay in the south, where they only like pious works and do not perceive the essence of buddhahood." Then Prajnatara gave Bodhidharma a verse of instruction:

> Traveling the road, crossing the water,
> you will meet a sheep.
> Going alone, without rest,
> you will cross the river in the dark.
> Under the sun, a nice pair—elephant and horse;
> Two young cinnamon trees will flourish forever.

He also said, "You will see someone in the woods who will realize enlightenment," and again he spoke in verse:

> Though China is vast, there is no other road.
> You need successors to follow in your footsteps.
> A golden rooster will be able to pick up a single grain
> And support all the saintly people in the world.

Having thus received confirmation and predictions in detail, Bodhidharma attended Prajnatara for forty years.

After Prajnatara died, another of his disciples, Buddhasena, having received Prajnatara's confirmation, taught as did Bodhidharma, but another disciple divided his followers into six sects. Bodhidharma taught and converted these six sects and became respected all over the land.

When over sixty years had passed in this manner, Bodhidharma knew that conditions were ripe for China, so he went to the rajah and said, "Respect the Buddha, the Teaching, and the Community, and benefit the people thereby. The conditions for me to go to China are ripe; I will come back when I have finished my work." The rajah wept and said, "What is wrong with this country? What is auspicious about that land? Anyway, when your task in China is done, come right back—don't forget the land of your parents." The rajah saw him off, accompanying him to the port.

Bodhidharma traveled by sea for three years, finally arriving in southern China in the year 527. Thus it was that he first had an audience with the Emperor Wu of the Liang dynasty in southern China. This was what Prajnatara had been referring to when he said, "Don't stay in the south."

From there Bodhidharma went north to the kingdom of Wei. It is said that he rode on a reed; people usually take this literally, so Bodhidharma is often portrayed standing on a reed, but this is wrong. A reed is a small boat shaped like a reed, not literally a reed. "You will meet a sheep" refers to Emperor Wu of Liang. "You will cross the river in the dark" refers to the Yangtze River, which separated the northern kingdom of Wei and the southern kingdom of Liang.

So Bodhidharma soon arrived at Shaolin monastery on Mount Song, where he stayed in the eastern hall. No one could figure him out, as he sat day and night. Because of this he was called the Indian Who Stares at the Wall. Thus did Bodhidharma spend nine years there without any noisy explanations, without hastily teaching.

After nine years, having bequeathed his "skin, flesh, bones, and marrow" to his four disciples Daofu, Daoyu, Congzhi, and Huike, he knew their potentials had matured.

At that time there were two deviants named Bodhiruci and precept master Guanglu, who were extremely upset to see master Bodhidharma's virtue spreading over the land and to see people trusting him and respecting him. They not only hurled stones at him knocking out his front teeth, they also tried to poison him five times. On their sixth attempt, Bodhidharma placed the poison on a boulder, and the boulder split.

Realizing his mission was over, he thought to himself, "I received the confirmation and prediction of my late teacher; I saw a great atmospheric phenomenon in China and knew for certain that there were people with the capacity for the great teaching. But since my meeting with Emperor Wu of Liang, I couldn't find anyone suitable. As I sat coolly doing nothing for nine years, I found only the great Huike, to whom I passed on the Way that I realized. Having done this task, my time is ended. Now I should leave." So saying, he sat up and passed away. He is buried on Bear Ear Mountain. It is said that he later met a man named Song Yun on the Su Range, but the fact is that he is buried on Bear Ear Mountain.

Based on the instruction and final direction of the Buddhist master Prajnatara, Bodhidharma became the founder of Zen in China. In the beginning of his acquaintance with Prajnatara, when he explained about the jewel, Prajnatara said, "What among all things is formless?" Bodhidharma said, "Nonorigination is formless." Even if you speak of empty silence, actually this is not formless. Therefore he said nonorigination is formless. Thus one would understand it as like a sheer cliff, one would understand it as being clear in everything, and recognize that everything is nothing else, just naturally abiding in its normal state—but this is not the unoriginated, so it is not formless.

Before heaven and earth are separated, how could holy and ordinary be distinguished? In this realm, there is not a single thing to appear, not a mote of dust that can defile. But it is not that there is originally nothing. Then you are empty and open, spiritually aware, wide awake and unbefuddled. Here there is nothing to compare, and never has anything accompanied it. Therefore it is the greatest of the great. That is why it is said that the great is called inconceivable, and the inconceivable is called the nature of reality.

Even a priceless jewel cannot compare with it; even the clear light of the mind cannot represent it. Therefore Bodhidharma said the jewel had a mundane luster and could not be considered supreme— the luster of wisdom is supreme. This is how he understood it. Though his explanation was truly from natural wisdom, yet he sat in meditation for seven days listening to the subtle teachings of meditation being explained to him, and thus developed supreme knowledge of the Way.

Thus we should know it is after meticulous discernment and complete arrival at such a state that you know the existence of what the Buddhas and Zen founders realized. Having clarified what the Buddhas of the past realized, one should be a descendant of the enlightened ones. This fact is particularly illustrated by this worthy— though he was already like one with natural wisdom, he went on to develop knowledge of the supreme Way. And after that, he also completely mastered the attention needed to preserve and maintain it in the future. He studied thoroughly over a period of forty years in attendance on Prajnatara, then passed sixty more years not forgetting Prajnatara's bequest for the future, and subsequently spent three years crossing the sea. At last he arrived in an unknown land, and while sitting coolly for nine years he found people with the capacity for the great teaching. Finally he was able to spread the true teaching of the Buddhas, thus requiting his debt to his teacher. His hardships were hardest of all, his austerities were most austere.

Students of Zen today, however, still want easy attainment even though the times are degenerate and people's capacities are inferior. I am afraid that people like this, the type who claim to attain what they have not, are conceited people who might as well withdraw from Zen study.

If you thoroughly penetrate the preceding story, you will know more and more how lofty it is. Breaking up your mind and abandoning your body, if you closely investigate the Way, there will be a subtle influence from the enlightened ones, and you will directly meet with what the enlightened ones realized. Don't think that a bit of knowledge or half an understanding is enough.

Again I have a humble saying:

There is no more location, no bounds, no outside—
Is there any thing at all, even in the slightest?

30

Huike
(Shenguang)

Huike studied with the Buddhist master Bodhidharma. One day he said to the master, "I have already ended all involvements." Bodhidharma said, "Doesn't that turn into nihilism?" Huike said, "No." Bodhidharma said, "How can you prove it?" Huike said, "I am always clearly aware. Therefore words cannot reach it." Bodhidharma said, "This is the essence of the mind, which all Buddhas realize—doubt no more."

Before Huike's parents had any children, his father used to think to himself, "We honor good in this house—why should we have no children?" He prayed for a long time, until one night he sensed a strange light illumining the room. That night his wife conceived Huike. As he was growing up, Huike was named Guang, "Light," because of the auspicious sign of the light filling the room on the night of his conception.

He had an extraordinary spirit even from childhood. He lived for a long time in the region of the ancient capital and read widely. He paid no attention to making a living, but liked to roam in the mountains and by the rivers. He used to lament, "The teachings of Confucius and Lao-tzu are rules for manners and arts; the book of Chuang-tzu and the *I Ching* still do not exhaust the subtle truth."

He was ordained as a Buddhist monk by a meditation master, then traveled around to lectures and studied all the principles of the individual and collective practices of Buddhism. One day while reading one of the scriptures on wisdom he felt a transcendent sense of satisfaction. For eight years after that he sat peacefully day and night. While in a state of profound calm and stillness he saw a spiritual being, which said to him, "You are about to realize the effect of your practice—why linger here? The Great Way is not far—go south." Realizing that it was spiritual help, he changed his name to Shenguang, "Spiritual Light."

The next day his head hurt as though it had been spiked. As his teacher tried to cure the pain, a voice from nowhere said, "This is the changing of bones—this is not an ordinary pain." Shenguang then told his teacher he had seen a spirit. His teacher looked at the crown of his head and saw lumps like five peaks standing out. He said, "Your features are auspicious—you will have realization. The spirit directing you south must have been referring to the great master Bodhidharma at Shaolin—he must be your teacher."

Receiving this instruction, Shenguang went to Shaolin monastery on Mount Song. This was in December of the year 528. The great teacher did not let him in, so Shenguang stood outside the window. That night a heavy snow fell. He stood in the snow, waiting for daybreak. The snow piled up, burying him to his waist, and the cold penetrated his bones. As he wept, each tear froze, making him even colder. He thought to himself, "When the ancients sought the Way, they broke their bones and extracted the marrow, shed their blood to appease the hunger of others, spread their hair over mud as a mat, hurled themselves from cliffs to feed tigers. If even the people of old did such things, what about me?" With these thoughts he spurred on his determination and stood there firmly, unflagging, without moving.

At dawn, the great master, seeing that Shenguang had been standing in the snow all night, took pity on him and asked him what he was seeking. He replied, "I only ask that the teacher open the gate of the elixir of universal compassion to liberate all beings." The great teacher said, "The supreme ineffable Way of all enlightened ones involves ages of effort, carrying out what is difficult to carry out, enduring what is difficult to endure. How can you hope for true religion with little virtue, little wisdom, a shallow heart, and an arrogant mind? It would just be a waste of effort."

So saying, Bodhidharma paid no more attention to him. Shenguang, hearing these merciful admonitions, wept even more, and his determination to see the Way became yet keener. He took a sharp sword and cut off his left arm. The great teacher then knew he had the capacity for the teaching, and said to him, "When the Buddhas first sought the Way, they forgot their bodies for the sake of truth. Now you have cut off your arm in my presence—you are capable of seeking."

Shenguang's name was therefore changed to Huike, which means "Wisdom and Capacity." Finally he was allowed to associate with Bodhidharma.

Huike spent eight years with Bodhidharma after that. Once he asked the great teacher, "Can I hear about the seal of truth of the Buddhas?" Bodhidharma said, "The seal of truth of the Buddhas is not gotten from another." Another time he instructed Huike, "Outwardly cease all involvements, inwardly have no coughing or sighing in the mind—with your mind like a wall you can enter the Way."

Huike was always talking about mind and nature, but he did not realize the essence of truth. The great teacher just refuted his errors and did not explain the essence of mind that is free from thought. In *Mystic Devices in the Room* it says, "One time Huike climbed up Few Houses Peak with Bodhidharma. Bodhidharma asked, 'Where are we going?' Huike said, 'Please go right ahead—that's it.' Bodhidharma said, 'If you go right ahead, you cannot move a step.' Hearing this, Huike was enlightened."

One time Huike said to Bodhidharma, "I have already ended all involvements," and he finally reached the point where he had no further doubt. Eventually Bodhidharma bequeathed both the robe and the teaching to him, saying, "Inwardly transmit the seal of truth for the realization of the enlightened mind; outwardly transmit the vestment to certify the religion." So after the great teacher died, the master Huike, succeeding him, spread the mystic way.

When he handed the teaching on to his successor Sengcan, Huike said, "I still have a burden from the past, which I must now make up for." Having transmitted his bequest, he went to the metropolis of Ye and taught when the occasion arose. All kinds of people, monks and nuns and lay people, reposed their faith in him. He spent thirty years in this way, hiding his light and mixing in with the crowd, changing his appearance. Sometimes he would go to the wine shops, sometimes to the butcher stalls. Sometimes he would give talks on the street, sometimes he would work along with the outhouse cleaners. Someone asked him, "You are a man of the Way—why do you act like this?" Huike said, "I tune my mind by myself—what business is it of yours?"

Later he preached at the gate of a certain monastery, and people gathered in droves. At that time a certain monk was lecturing on the Nirvana Scripture in that monastery, but the people attending his lectures were gradually drawn to Huike's talks, and the monk could not contain his anger. He slandered Huike to a local official, and the official, fooled by what the monk said, unjustly persecuted Huike. Huike submitted without complaint and was executed in the year 593.

Now to begin with there is no distinction of superiority and inferiority among the Buddhist masters in their honorable virtues, but this master was great among the great ones. Even though Bodhidharma came from India, Zen could not have reached the present day had it not been for Huike's transmission. His trials were greater than others, his determination in seeking surpassed all.

And Bodhidharma, waiting for a genuine student, did not speak for a long time and did not especially give any teachings to his successor. He just said, "Outwardly cease all involvements, inwardly have no coughing or sighing in the mind—with your mind like a wall you can enter the Way."

In truth, if you stop thinking you will expose the essence of mind. Hearing this, you may try to become mindless like a wall, but this is not really seeing the mind. Thus Huike said, "I am always clearly aware." If you can be like this, this is what the Buddhas all realize.

So if you stop all involvement with objects outside, there will be no thoughts within. Wide awake, you will be unmuddled—clearly aware, it is originally apparent. Here there is no distinction between old and new or past and present, no separation between self and other. By harmonization with the realization of Buddhas, the mental communication of the Zen founders passed through India to China and joined China to Japan. It was so in the past and it is so today. Don't just long for the past—avail yourself of the present day to practice Zen. Don't think it has been a long time since the Buddha—don't give up on yourself, understand and clarify yourself.

As usual, I have a humble saying:

Empty yet radiantly bright, conditioned thought ended,
Perspicuous, aware, always open and clear.

31

Sengcan

Sengcan said to the Zen master Huike, "I am riddled with sickness; please absolve me of my sin." Huike said, "Bring me your sin and I will absolve you." After a long pause, Sengcan said, "When I look for my sin I cannot find it." Huike said, "I have absolved you. You should live by the Buddha, the Teaching, and the Community."

It is not known where Sengcan came from. When he visited Zen master Huike, he was a layman over forty years of age. He did not say his name, but came to the Zen master and asked for relief from his illness, as told in the story.

When Huike told him to live by the Buddha, the Teaching, and the Community, Sengcan said, "I can see you are a monk, a member of the Buddhist community; what are the Buddha and the Teaching?" Huike said, "This mind is Buddha, this mind is the Teaching; the Teaching and the Buddha are not separate. This is also true of the Community."

Sengcan said, "Today for the first time I have realized that the essence of sin is not inside, not outside, not in between. So it is also of mind. Buddha and the Teaching are not separate either." Huike regarded him as having the capacity for the teaching, so he had him ordained as a monk and named him Sengcan, which means "Light of the Religious Community." After this his sickness gradually healed.

Sengcan attended Huike for two years. Then Huike said to him,

"The great teacher Bodhidharma came here to China from India, and gave me both the robe and the teaching. Now I entrust them to you." He also said, "Although you have attained the teaching, for the time being you should go into the mountains and not teach publicly. There will be trouble in this country."

Sengcan said, "Since you know about this, please give me some instructions." Huike said, "It is not that I know—this is the prediction given to Bodhidharma by Prajnatara, who said, 'Inside the heart is auspicious, but outside is bad luck.' According to my calculations, this prediction refers to your generation. Think about these words and don't get caught up in worldly problems."

After that Sengcan lived in seclusion in the mountains for ten years. This was the time that the Martial Emperor of the Wei dynasty persecuted the Buddhist religion. Because of this Sengcan changed his appearance and stayed in the mountains, dwelling in no fixed place.

While in this condition Sengcan met the novice Daoxin, who was to become his successor. He said to Daoxin, "After my teacher transmitted Zen to me, he went to the big city and spent thirty years there. Now that I have found you, why should I stay here?" Then he went to another mountain, but later returned to his old abode. The local people flocked to him and offered him support. He gave extensive explanations of the essence of mind for the people, then at a religious meeting he died under a tree. His Poem on the Trust in the Heart was recorded and circulates even today. Later he was given the title Master of Mirrorlike Knowledge.

The sickness plaguing him in his first meeting with Huike was leprosy. But as he associated with the Zen master, his sickness disappeared. There is nothing special about this story: understanding that the nature of sin is ungraspable, he realized that the nature of mind is originally pure. Thus he heard that the Buddha and the Truth are not separate, that mind and reality are *thus*. When you really know the original mind, there is no difference in dying in one place and being born in another—how much less could there be any distinction of sin and virtue there! Thus the body-mind after all does not exist; we are fundamentally free from skin, flesh, bones, and marrow. Therefore his disease disappeared and his original mind appeared.

In expounding the essence of the teaching, Sengcan said, "The supreme Way is without difficulty—it is only averse to discrimination." In conclusion he said, "There is no way to talk about it—it is not of the past, future, or present." Really there is no inside or outside, no in between—what would you choose, what reject? You cannot take, you cannot leave. Once you have no hate or love, you are empty and clear. At no time do you lack, nothing is extra.

Yet even so, investigate thoroughly to reach the point of ungraspability, to arrive at the realm of ungraspability. Without becoming nihilistic, not being like wood or stone, you should be able to "strike space and make an echo, tie lightning to make a form." Carefully observe the realm where there are no tracks or traces, yet don't hide there. If you can be like this, even though "*that* is not the present phenomena, it is not within reach of ear or eye," you should see without hindrance, you should comprehend without deviation.

Can we add a discerning word to this story?

Essential emptiness has no inside or outside—
Sin and virtue leave no traces there.
Mind and Buddha are fundamentally *thus*;
The Teaching and Community are clear.

32

Daoxin

Daoxin said to the Zen master Sengcan, "I beg your compassion—please give me a way of liberation." Sengcan said, "Who is binding you?" Daoxin said, "No one is binding me." Sengcan said, "Then why seek liberation?" At these words Daoxin was greatly enlightened.

Daoxin, succeeding to the Way of the Zen founders, concentrated his mind without sleeping and never lay down for sixty years. In 617 he came to Qi province with a group of followers. At that time an army of bandits had been besieging the city for seventy days, and all the people were in terror. Daoxin, feeling pity for them, taught them to recite the name of great transcendent wisdom. When the bandits looked over the outer city wall, there seemed to be a supernatural army; they said to each other that there must be someone extraordinary in the city and they shouldn't attack it. Gradually they left.

In 624 Daoxin returned to Qi. That spring he stayed on Broken Head Mountain, where students gathered in great numbers. One day he met his future successor Hongren on the road to Huangmei, and he also produced a collateral branch of the teaching on Ox Head Mountain.

In 643 the emperor of China heard of Daoxin and wanted to see him, so he summoned him to the capital. Daoxin refused three times and finally excused himself on account of illness. The fourth time, the emperor instructed his emissary to take the Zen master's head if he continued to refuse. When the emissary came and told Daoxin about this, the master just stretched out his neck to the sword, remaining fully composed. The emissary thought this remarkable and returned to report it to the emperor. The emperor admired the Zen master all the more; he sent him some rare cloth and let him have his way.

In 651 Daoxin suddenly admonished his disciples, "All things are liberated. You should keep mindful of this and teach it in the future." So saying, he passed away while sitting peacefully. He was seventy-two years old. He was entombed on the mountain where he lived. The next year the door of the mausoleum opened of itself for no reason; the Zen master looked just as he had when he was alive. After that his disciples did not dare to shut the tomb. Later he was posthumously entitled Great Physician Zen Master.

Although there is actually no superiority or inferiority in the practice of the Zen masters, this one followed the religion of emptiness from boyhood, just as though he had studied it in a former lifetime. Throughout his life he never associated with rulers or politicians. He practiced the Way with single-minded determination, never turning back. In the very beginning he declared the way of liberation, and he also opened the gate of liberation when he was about to die, to let people know that life and death do not bind us. He really was an extraordinary man, the kind met once in a thousand years.

The cultivation of emptiness is called the gate of liberation. Why is this? Neither sentience nor buddhahood binds you—what more birth and death could there be to entangle you? This cannot be assessed through body or mind, it cannot be discerned by illusion or enlightenment. Even if you talk about mind, objects, afflictions, and enlightenment, all these are different names for the self. Therefore mountains and rivers have no barriers, subject and object are not different. Because of this, "When it's cold it chills you thoroughly, when it's hot it heats you thoroughly."

Then when you cross this barrier, it is not this principle either. That is to say, there is neither bondage nor liberation, neither that nor this. Things do not set up names, things do not separate their forms.

Therefore deliberate cultivation comes to an end; how can it have anything to do with relative and absolute? There is no sitting upright in the hall; do not rest in duality. If you can see in this way, you do not even use the word liberation, much less complain of bondage.

Furthermore, you actually have a light called vision of the world, you have a sense of taste called blending the six flavors. Therefore you emanate light everywhere and prepare a feast everywhere. As you savor it, you find rich flavor where there is no flavor. As you observe it, you find true form where there is no form. Thus there are no rulers or politicians to approach, there is no physical or mental sitting or reclining.

If you can reach this state, you are the Zen master, the Zen master is you. Is this not what is meant by the saying that everything is liberation? Is this not transmitting the teaching to the future? The seamless monument will suddenly open its doors, and the ordinary appearance will be revealed.

Again I have a humble saying:

When mind is empty, pure knowledge has no wrong or right;
Here I don't know what there is to bind or free.
Even if you distinguish the elements of body and mind,
Seeing, hearing, sound and form, are ultimately not another.

33

Hongren

Hongren met the Zen master Daoxin on a road in Huangmei. The Zen master asked him what his name was; he replied, "I have an essence, but it is not a common name." The Zen master said, "What name is it?" He replied, "It is the essence of buddhahood." The Zen master said, "Have you no name?" He said, "None, because essence is empty." The Zen master recognized his capacity for truth, and passed the teaching and the robe on to him.

Hongren was formerly an itinerant forester who planted trees. He once asked the Zen master Daoxin to tell him about Zen, but the Zen master said, "You are already old. Even if you learned about Zen, how could you spread the teaching? If you come back, I will wait for you."

The forester then went to a young woman washing her clothes by the river and asked her, "Can I stay for a while?" The woman said, "Go ask my father and brother." He said, "If you agree, I'll go." The woman shook her head in agreement, and the old man left. Then the woman returned home, and subsequently found she was pregnant. Her parents were outraged and drove her out of their home. Having no place to go, by days she did spinning for hire and at night she stayed at an inn.

Finally the young woman gave birth to a son. She considered him an ill omen and threw him in the river. The infant, however, went against the current and did not get wet. For seven days spiritual beings protected him and prevented any harm from coming to him: by day two birds came and covered the infant with their wings, and by night two dogs curled up around him. The infant was fresh and clean, and had all of his faculties. His mother, now regarding him as a marvel, at length took him in and raised him. As a child he begged with his mother, and people called him the boy without a surname.

Later he met the Zen master Daoxin on a road in Huangmei, one day when the Zen master had gone out for a walk. The master saw that the boy was unusual, and asked him what his name was. Ultimately the Zen master recognized him as one with the capacity for Zen teaching, so he asked the boy's mother to allow him to leave home and become a disciple. At that time he was seven years old.

From the time Hongren thus received initiation and became a monk, he sat in meditation all the time, except when he was doing his chores. Finally in the year 675 he announced to his own students that he had finished his work and was going to leave. So saying, he passed away as he sat.

There is a name that is not received from one's father, not received from one's ancestors, not inherited from Buddhas, not inherited from Zen masters; it is called the buddha nature, or essence of buddhahood. Zen study is basically to reach the fundamental and clarify the essence of mind. If you don't reach the fundamental, you live and die in vain, misunderstanding yourself and others. As for what this fundamental essence is, your features may differ as you die and are born over and over again, but at all times there is an inherent awareness.

This can be known from the present story—having sought the Way as the pine planter in the past, now receiving the transmission of the robe and the teaching as a seven-year-old boy, from then to now the mind hasn't changed on account of birth, the essence hasn't changed on account of physical form. In Zen master Hongzhi's eulogy of Hongren it says, "Before and after, two bodies; past and present, one mind." Though bodies change, there is no separate mind, past or present. You should know that since countless eons past it has just been *thus*.

If you arrive at this fundamental essence, it cannot be distinguished in terms of caste or class. Because people of all classes have the same essence, because the fundamental essence is *thus*, when people of any caste are ordained as Buddhist monks or nuns, they are all known by the surname Shakya, the family name of Buddha, to let it be known that there is no distinction among them.

This means that really there is no gap between you and me. It is just that we have the appearance of self and other, just like former and later bodies. But if you cannot discern this and cannot understand the mind, you erroneously think of self and environment as separate, and distinguish your own being from the being of others. Because of this you have emotional attachments to all kinds of things and are confused all the time. But once you realize this realm, even if you change your form and transform your life, how could that block the self or change the mind?

This should be known from the itinerant forester and the boy. He was born without a father, so we should know that people are not necessarily born of the bloodline of a father and mother. Thus, although according to the view of emotional attachments the physical body is received from one's parents, still we should realize that our being is not the gross physical elements.

If you understand the body in this way, then there is nothing at all accompanying the self, and at no time is there any difference from oneself. That is why an ancient said, "All beings have always been absorbed in the essence of reality." If you can comprehend this Way and practice this Way, you will meet Zen master Daoxin and be equal to Zen master Hongren. There will be no difference between countries or between times.

Now how can I make a comment that will accord with this principle?

The moon bright, the water pure, the autumn sky is clear;
How could there be a fleck of cloud spotting this great clarity?

34

Huineng

Huineng worked in the mill at Huangmei, where the Zen master Hongren was teaching. One night the Zen master came to the mill and asked Huineng, "Is the rice white yet?" Huineng said, "It's white, but hasn't been sifted." The Zen master knocked the mortar three times with his staff; Huineng shook rice in a sieve three times, and entered the Zen master's room.

During the first quarter of the seventh century Huineng's father was demoted and sent to the southern frontier region, where he settled down. After his father died, Huineng was raised by his mother. As he was growing up his family was extremely poor, and he eked out a living by cutting wood.

One day when Huineng went to market with a bundle of wood, he heard a traveler reciting the Diamond Cutter Scripture. When the traveler reached the part where it says, "You should activate the mind without dwelling on anything," Huineng experienced enlightenment. He said to the traveler, "What scripture is this? Who did you learn it from?" The traveler said, "It is called the Diamond Cutter Scripture, and I learned it from the great teacher Hongren in Huangmei."

Huineng told his mother that he intended to seek a teacher for the truth. He went to another district and became friends with a high-minded man named Liu Zhilue. Liu's mother-in-law was a nun who constantly recited the Nirvana Scripture. After listening to the scripture for a while, Huineng expounded its meaning. The nun then picked up a volume of the scripture and asked about certain words. Huineng said, "I can't read—ask me about the meaning." The nun said, "If you can't read, how can you understand the meaning?" Huineng said, "The subtle principles of Buddha are not bound up in written words." This startled the nun, who told the elders of the town, "This is a man of the Way. We should invite him to stay here and offer him support." After that the people who lived there came in droves to see him and pay their respects.

In the vicinity there was an ancient temple site; the people decided to rebuild it and invite Huineng to stay there. Monks, nuns, and lay people gathered in large numbers, and it soon became a sanctuary. One day Huineng thought to himself, "I seek the great teaching—why should I stop halfway?" The next day he left.

When he reached a certain cliffside cave in another district, he met meditation master Zhiyuan, from whom he requested more instruction. Zhiyuan said, "You have an unusually serene appearance, not like that of ordinary people. I have heard that the Indian Bodhidharma transmitted the mind seal, and that it has been handed down to Hongren, who lives at Huangmei. You should go there to seek certainty."

Huineng thanked him and left. Then he went directly to Huangmei and called on the Zen master Hongren. The Zen master said, "Where do you come from?" Huineng said, "From the south." The master said, "What are you seeking?" Huineng said, "I just seek to be a Buddha." The master said, "Southerners have no buddha nature—how can you attain buddhahood?" Huineng said, "As far as people are concerned, there are north and south, but how could that apply to the buddha nature?" The Zen master knew he was not an ordinary man, and sent him to the rice-pounding quarters of the monastery mill. Huineng went to work pounding rice. For eight months he worked without rest.

Eventually, realizing the time for transmission had come, Zen master Hongren said to the assembly, "The truth is hard to understand. Don't uselessly memorize my words and take that as your own responsibility. Each of you should freely compose a verse; if the meaning of the words is in accord with truth, I'll give you the robe and the teaching."

At that time Shenxiu was the eldest of the more than seven hundred monks in the community. He was versed in both social and mystic sciences, and was admired by all. They all deferred to him, reasoning that if he couldn't write an appropriate verse then none of them could. Shenxiu heard the praise of the community and reflected no further. Having composed a verse, he went several times to present it, but he felt faint and broke out in a sweat, unable to present the verse. Over a period of four days he tried and failed thirteen times to present his verse. Finally he thought that it would be better to write it on the wall of the hall. If the Zen master thought it was satisfactory, he would come forth and say it was his work. If the master thought it unsatisfactory, he would go pass the years in the mountains—why practice anymore, receiving the homage of others?

That night at midnight, when no one would know, Shenxiu took a lamp and went into the south hall, where he wrote his verse on a wall, expressing his insight:

> The body is the tree of enlightenment,
> The mind like a clear mirror stand;
> Time and again wipe it diligently,
> Don't let it gather dust.

The next day as the Zen master was walking around he saw the verse. Knowing it had been composed by Shenxiu, he praised it, saying, "If later generations practice in accord with this, they too will realize an excellent result." He then had everyone memorize it.

Hearing this verse recited in the mill, Huineng asked a student, "What writing is this?" The student told Huineng what had transpired. Huineng had him recite the verse again; after a silence, Huineng then said, "It's very nice, all right, but it's not perfect." The student scolded him, "What does a common sort like you know? Don't talk like a madman." Huineng said, "You don't believe me? I'd like to add a verse to this." The student just looked at him without answering and laughed.

That night Huineng took a servant boy with him to the hall. Huineng held a lamp while he had the boy write another verse next to that of Shenxiu:

Enlightenment is basically not a tree,
And the clear mirror not a stand.
Fundamentally there is not a single thing—
Where can dust collect?

Seeing this verse, everybody on the mountain said it was the work of a living saint, and everyone praised it. The Zen master, knowing it was Huineng's verse, said, "Who composed this? It is someone who has not perceived his real nature yet." So saying, he erased the verse. Because of this, the community ignored it thereafter.

That night the Zen master secretly came to Huineng in the mill and said, "Is the rice white yet?" Huineng said, "It's white, but hasn't been sifted." The master struck the mortar thrice; then Huineng sifted some rice three times and entered the Zen master's room. The master told him, "For the sake of the one great matter of the appearance of enlightened knowledge in the world, the Buddhas guide people in accord with their capacities. Eventually there came to be teachings of ten stages, three vehicles, sudden and gradual enlightenment, and so on. Moreover, the Buddha transmitted the supreme, extremely subtle, esoteric real treasury of the eye of the right teaching of complete enlightenment to his senior disciple Kasyapa the Elder. This was handed on until it reached Bodhidharma in the twenty-eighth generation; he came to China and found the great master Huike. Then it continued to be transmitted until it came to me. Now I pass on to you the treasure of the teaching and the robe that has been handed down. Preserve the teaching well and do not let it be cut off."

Kneeling, Huineng received the robe and the teaching. Then he asked, "I have received the teaching—to whom should the robe be imparted?" The Zen master Hongren said, "A long time ago when Bodhidharma first came to China, people didn't believe in Zen, so he handed on the robe as an indication of having attained the teaching. Now faith has developed, whereas the robe has become a source of contention. Therefore let it stop with you—don't pass it on. Now you should go far away and conceal yourself until the appropiate time to teach comes. It is said that the life of a man who has received this robe hangs like a thread."

Huineng said, "Where should I hide?" Hongren said, "When you come to Huai, stop there; when you come to Hui, hide there for a while."

Huineng then paid his respects and left with the robe. Zen master Hongren personally escorted him to the crossing at the foot of Mount Huangmei. Then Huineng saluted him and said, "You should go back now. I have already realized the Way, and should ferry myself over." Hongren said, "Though you have attained the Way, still I will ferry you over." So saying, he took the boat pole and crossed over to the other shore with Huineng. Then Hongren went back to the monastery alone. The community had no knowledge of this.

After that, the Zen master did not lecture any more. When people came and questioned him, he said, "My Way has gone." Someone asked, "Who has got your robe and teaching?" Hongren said, "The able one got them."

Then the people reasoned that he must be referring to Huineng, because *neng* means "able." But when they looked for him, they found that he was gone. They realized that he had gotten the robe and the teaching, so they set out after him.

At that time there was a monk there named Huiming, who had been a general in the army. He led the expedition in pursuit of Huineng and overtook him on the Dayu Range.

Huineng said, "This robe symbolizes faith—why fight over it?" He put the robe and bowl on a boulder and hid in the bush. When Huiming arrived, he tried to pick up the robe and bowl, but he was unable to budge them even though he tried with all his strength. Then Huiming trembled and said, "I have come for the teaching, not for a robe."

Now Huineng came out and sat on the boulder. Huiming bowed and said, "Please reveal the essence of the teaching to me." Huineng said, "When you don't think of good or evil, what is your original face?" Huiming was greatly enlightened at these words. He then asked, "Is there any further secret meaning beyond what you have just said?" Huineng said, "What I have told you is not a secret; if you look into your mind, the secret is in you." Huiming said, "Although I was with Hongren at Huangmei, I didn't truly realize my own likeness. Now that I have received your teaching, I am like one who drinks water and knows firsthand whether it is cool or warm. You are my teacher." Huineng said, "If it is as you say, Hongren is your teacher as well as mine."

Huiming then bowed in thanks and left. Later, when he became an abbot, he changed his name to Daoming, avoiding the use of Hui out of deference to Huineng. When anyone came to study with him, he would always send them to call on Huineng.

After Huineng received the robe and the teaching, he concealed himself for ten years among hunters in the forest. In 676 he came to Nanhai in southern China, where he found doctrinal master Yinzong lecturing on the Nirvana Scripture at Faxing temple. Huineng stood in the hallway for a while. A strong wind was blowing the temple banner, and he overheard two monks arguing, one saying that the flag was moving, the other that the wind was moving. They argued back and forth without getting to the truth, so Huineng said, "May a layman interrupt your lofty discussion? It is not the wind or the flag that is moving—your minds are moving."

Hearing these words, Yinzong was amazed. The next day he called Huineng to him and asked about the meaning of the wind and the flag. Huineng gave him a thorough explanation of the principle. Then Yinzong unconsciously stood up and said, "You are definitely not an ordinary man. Who is your teacher?" Concealing nothing any longer, Huineng told him how he had attained the teaching. Then Yinzong became his disciple and asked to receive instruction in the essentials of Zen. He said to the assembly in the temple, "I am an ordinary mortal, but now I have met a living saint." Then he pointed to Huineng in the crowd and said, "This is he." They asked him to bring out the robe of the faith that had been transmitted to him, so that everyone could look upon it.

On the fifteenth day of January, several famous priests were assembled to formally ordain Huineng, and on February eighth he received the precepts from a preceptor. The altar on which this ceremony took place had been set up by the fifth-century doctrinal master and translator Gunabhadra, who wrote in his record of the event, "Later there will be a living saint who will receive the precepts at this altar." Also, in the late sixth century the doctrinal master Paramartha personally planted a bodhi tree on either side of the altar and told the community, "In one hundred and twenty years there will be a great enlightened man who will expound the unexcelled religion under these trees and will liberate countless people." After having received the precepts, Huineng began to teach Zen under these trees, as though in fulfillment of the prophecy.

The next year, on the eighth of February, Huineng suddenly said to the community, "I don't want to stay here—I want to go back to my old hiding place." So Yinzong and over a thousand monks, nuns, and lay people escorted him back to Baolin monastery in Canton. The inspector of the province invited him to teach at Dafan temple, and also received the formless precepts of the mind ground from him. His disciples recorded his sayings there and called this record the Altar Scripture, which now is popular. After that he returned to Caoqi and showered the rain of the great teaching. Those who were awakened were not less than a thousand. Finally Huineng passed away sitting, at the age of seventy-six.

At the time of the transmission of the teaching, the Zen master Hongren said, "Is the rice white yet?" These grains of rice are the spiritual sprouts of the monarch of truth—the life root of the sages and ordinary people. Once in a wild field, they grow by themselves even without hoeing. Husked and polished, they take on no defilement. Yet even being so, they still have not been sifted and strained. If you sift and strain them, you will comprehend inside and out, you will be free in all ways. As the Zen master knocked the mortar thrice, the rice grains spontaneously arrayed themselves and the mind potential suddenly was revealed. As Huineng shook the rice in the strainer three times, the Zen Way was communicated. Since that time, the night of the knocking of the mortar has never dawned, the day of the transmission has never ended.

Let us reflect on this. The great master Huineng had been a wood-cutter from the far south of China; he used to roam the mountains with his axe, and had no scholastic learning. Yet when he heard just one line of a scripture, the mind that does not dwell on anything arose in him. Later he labored in a mill with mortar and pestle. Though he had no experience of formal Zen study, after only eight months of diligent work, as he had illumined the mind like a clear mirror that is not a stand, the transmission was carried out in the middle of the night, and the lifeline of the Zen founders was passed on. While it does not necessarily depend on many years of effort, it is clear that he exerted the utmost diligence and care. The enlightenment of the Buddhas basically cannot be measured in terms of long or short time—how can the transmission of the Way of the Zen founders be understood in terms of divisions of past and present?

Furthermore, I have spoken this way and that for ninety days over this summer retreat, commenting on past and present, explaining the enlightened ones with both coarse words and soft speech. Entering into the subtle and the minute, falling into two and three, I have defiled the Way of Zen and exposed the disgrace of the school. Thus I think you people have all understood the principle and have gained strength, but it seems you have not personally accorded with the meaning of the Zen founders. Your practice is not like that of the sages of the past.

We are lucky to have been able to meet like this. If you work on the Way single-mindedly, you should be able to master it, but many of you have not reached the shore. You still cannot see into the inner sanctum. The time of Buddha is in the distant past, your work on the Way is not yet complete, and physical life is impossible to guarantee. How can you procrastinate? The end of the summer retreat is already at hand, and it is time to disband. How could you arbitrarily memorize a word or half a phrase and call that my teaching? Would you bring out a mere bit of knowledge, half an understanding, and call that what we are conveying here? Even if you have fully attained that power, the disgrace of the house will still be exposed—how much the more so if you wrongly expound the Way! If you want to truly arrive at this realm, you should not squander the time and should not use your body and mind arbitrarily.

As before, I have a humble saying to explain this story:

Knocking the mortar—the sound is high, beyond the sky;
Sifting in the clouds—the bright moon is clear deep in the
  night.

35

Qingyuan

Qingyuan went to study with the Zen master Huineng and asked, "What work is to be done so as not to fall into stages?" The Zen master inquired, "What have you done?" Qingyuan said, "I do not even practice the holy truths." The Zen master said, "What stage do you fall into?" Qingyuan said, "If I do not even practice the holy truths, what stages are there?" The Zen master recognized his profound capacity.

Qingyuan became a monk as a boy, and used to keep silent during discussions of the Way. Subsequently he heard of the teaching of Zen master Huineng and went there to study. He asked what is to be done so as not to fall into stages, and the Zen master recognized his profound capacity. Although Huineng had many disciples, Qingyuan was the foremost. It was the same as when Bodhidarma said that Huike had attained his marrow, even though Huike said nothing in response to a question about what he had realized.

One day the Zen master said to Qingyuan, "Since ancient times the robe and the teaching have been passed on together from teacher to apprentice. The robe represents faith, while the teaching stamps the mind. Now that I have found suitable people, why worry that they will not be believed? Ever since I received the robe I have had a lot of trouble, and there will surely be even more competitiveness in later generations. Therefore the robe will be left in this monastery as a keepsake. You should spread the teaching and not let it die out."

Having received the teaching, Qingyuan became a guide in his own right, during the lifetime of his predecessor Huineng. After he accepted Shitou as a disciple, many of the followers of Huineng came to him. He was the glory of Huineng's school. In 740 he announced his death and passed away sitting in the lotus posture.

Qingyuan's practice—refraining from discussion of the Way with others, keeping silent—was truly extraordinary. With this power of directed attention he asked Zen master Huineng what work does not fall into stages. He truly had subtle insight and was free from contrivance.

The Zen master wanted him to arrive at realization quickly, so he asked him what he had done. Qingyuan's acuity manifested itself as he replied that he did not even practice the holy truths. This is hearing what is hard to hear, meeting what is hard to meet. Even if contrivance ends, there is still some preservation of the self; if you are like this you make the mistake of falling into the deep pit of liberation, so this state has always been called religious attachment. Yunmen referred to it as the two kinds of sickness of the spiritual body. This comes from not having thoroughly passed through this point.

Therefore Qingyuan did not just realize the fundamental, he passed through this barrier. This is why the Zen master asked him what stage he would fall into. Truly in the realm of recondite mystery there is no more outside or inside; nothing can analyze the sphere of the profound ultimate. Therefore Qingyuan said, "What stages are there?" Having penetrated this state unclouded he reached the limits of investigation, so he said, "If I don't even practice the holy truths, what stages are there?"

In reality, even if you try to set up stages, fundamentally there are no boundaries in the void—where can you put a ladder? Those who interpret this point literally have since ancient times fallen into the view that all things are null and have formed the understanding that all things are annihilated. Qingyuan said he didn't even practice the holy truths—how could he linger in the voidness of things?

Observe closely—this realm of open clarity is brighter than the morning sun. Though this spiritual, immaterial true nature is not perceptual discrimination, it has comprehensive, perfectly lucid knowledge. Though it does not have bones or marrow, it has a clear luminous body that conceals nothing. This body cannot be discerned through motion or stillness, this knowledge cannot be discerned by conscious cognition. Yet because cognition is also this knowledge, motion and stillness are not something else either.

Therefore even the saints who go by stages up to the tenth and highest stage still do not see the buddha nature clearly. The Buddha said that this is because they still maintain that the teachings have objective reality and they still set up practice, and therefore their vision of buddha nature is still not clear. Because Buddhas ultimately have no practice and do not have spiritual stages, they see the buddha nature with perfect clarity.

In the twelfth book of the Nirvana Scripture it says, "Although innumerable saints fully practice the six ways of transcendence and the ten stages of enlightenment, they still cannot see their inherent buddha nature. Therefore the Buddha has said that they lack perception. Thus even if the state of saints has reached the tenth stage, they still do not clearly know or see the buddha nature. How much less can disciples or conditionally awakened people see it?"

So without relying on seeing and hearing, not being involved in knowing objects, try to see what is underneath. There will be an alert, awake knowledge that is not gotten from others; you will unexpectedly have a spontaneous realization.

Now how can I add a word to this story? Coming to this point, if you can add a word to this story, then you can make a tongueless man speak. If you can hear this principle, then you can make the transcendent being within you hear without ears and nod in understanding.

Coming and going on the bird's path, there are no tracks—
How can you look for stages on the mystic road?

36

Shitou

Shitou called on Zen master Qingyuan, who asked him, "Where have you come from?" Shitou said, "From Caoqi (where Zen master Huineng taught)." Qingyuan held up a whisk and said, "Is there this at Caoqi?" Shitou said, "Not only not at Caoqi—not even in India." Qingyuan said, "You haven't been to India, have you?" Shitou said, "If I had, it would be there." Qingyuan said, "That's not enough—say more." Shitou said, "You too should say a half—don't rely entirely on me." Qingyuan said, "I don't decline to speak to you, but I am afraid that later on no one will get it." Shitou said, "It is not that they won't get it, but no one can say it." Qingyuan hit Shitou with the whisk, whereupon Shitou experienced a great enlightenment.

Shitou is known for having stopped animal sacrifices among hunting people in his area when he was just a youth. He went to see the Zen master Huineng at Caoqi when he was only fourteen years old; he was initiated, but not yet ordained. When Huineng was about to pass on, he directed Shitou to go study with Qingyuan.

One day Qingyuan held up a whisk and said, "Is there this at Caoqi?" Shitou said, "Not only not at Caoqi—not even in India." In ancient as well as recent times they have held up the whisk to show a clue or introduction, to initiate action, to make people abandon sidetracks, or to give people immediate direction. Qingyuan also did this

as a test. But Shitou didn't yet understand what Qingyuan was calling "this," and still fixed his eyes on the raising of the whisk, saying,
"Not only not at Caoqi—not even in India."

In the raising of the whisk, what "Caoqi" or "India" can you establish? But such a view is still a verbal understanding of the objective
environment, so Qingyuan pressed him, saying, "You haven't been
to India, have you?" Shitou still didn't understand this remark, and
without forgetting himself he said, "If I had, it would be there."
Even though you have spoken of it, if you don't know it exists you
are not suitable. Therefore Qingyuan said, "That's not enough—say
more." He really acted with great kindness and compassion, giving
detailed indications in this way.

Here Shitou had no place to put himself, so he said, "You too
should say half—don't rely entirely on me." Having met and talked
thus, if they both transmitted a half, how could the whole thing be
said? Even if the universe crumbles and the whole essence is exposed
alone, this is still only halfway. Even this point is arrived at on one's
own, without depending on the arts of another; needless to say, ad-
vancing a step beyond the halfway point, subtly conveying a secret
message, doesn't depend on anything at all. How can someone else
know?

It is simply that it has always been inherent in oneself. Therefore
Qingyuan said, "I don't decline to say it to you, but I'm afraid that
later on no one will get it." Even if you speak of pain and bitterness,
if the other has no experience of pain piercing his bones or of bitterness splitting his tongue, in the end there is no way to convey it.
Therefore there will be no way to get it through words.

Because this is so, teachers do not speak at random and do not act
arbitrarily; they are careful in this way. But Shitou still didn't know
there was a subtle point conveyed, something that is not a partner of
things. Unable to perceive subtly, he said, "It is not that they won't
get it, but no one can say it." Shitou may say so, but upon reaching
this realm how can someone have nothing to say? If you reach this
realm, what will you get? He was still looking outside, estranged
from inner realization: therefore, in order to make him speedily re-

alize such a thing exists, to get him to know his original head right away, Qingyuan hit him with the whisk—he "beat the grass to frighten the snakes." Thus Shitou was greatly awakened.

By way of this story you should thoroughly examine learned knowledge and true realization, in order to arrive at the point where you can discern exactly which is which. When Shitou said, "Not only not at Caoqi—not even in India," he succeeded in breaking open heaven and earth and revealing the whole unique being, but he still had the affliction of self-consciousness. It was because of this that he could speak so grandiosely. But in the end, having perceived the revealing of the whole being at the raising of the whisk, at the blow of the whisk he knew it exists.

Zen students of recent times fruitlessly run around in the midst of sound and form, searching in seeing and hearing. Even if they have memorized the words of the Buddha and the Zen masters and have formulated some way of understanding to cling to, even if they say "not at Caoqi, not even in India," still they have realized nothing. If you are this way, then even if you have shaved your heads and put on robes so that outwardly you resemble the Buddha in appearance, you'll never escape the bonds of the prison of this world. How will you be able to halt the routines of mundane life? What a pity it is that people like this have vainly hung the monastic robe on a piece of wood. As the Buddha said, "They are not Buddhists—they have no name—they are no different from pieces of wood." That's what this means. Vainly squandering the donations of the faithful all your lives, in the end when you have to swallow a bitter pill you'll surely have many regrets.

So, having thoroughly investigated and penetrated through, if you reach the point where the whole being is revealed alone, as Shitou did when he first arrived, you will realize the nonexistence of either Caoqi or India. Where can one come or go? At this stage of vision, one does not wear the patchwork robe in vain. All the more so was this true of Shitou when at the blow of the whisk he realized the fact of being, and both forgot himself and also knew himself. He came to life in the midst of death; in the dark his true eye was illumined. This is the inner reality under the patchwork robe.

One time, as Shitou was reading a famous Buddhist treatise, he came to the point where it says, "It seems that only a sage can understand that myriad things are oneself." At this point he hit the desk and said, "A sage has no self, yet there is nothing that is not the self. The body of reality is formless—who speaks of self and other? The round mirror is marvelously bright—all things and the mysteries of their beings appear in it spontaneously. Objects and knowledge are not one—who says they come or go to one another? How true are the words of this treatise!" Then he rolled up the scroll and unexpectedly fell asleep. He dreamed he was riding with Zen master Huineng on a turtle swimming around in a deep lake. When he awoke he realized what it meant: the miraculous turtle was knowledge, the lake was the ocean of essence. "The Zen master and I were riding on spiritual knowledge floating on the ocean of essence." Subsequently he wrote *The Merging of Difference and Sameness*, which became popular.

Such a dream occurred to him because his spiritual knowledge was already equal to that of the Zen master Huineng and no different from that of Zen master Qingyuan. Moreover, one time in a lecture he said, "My teaching is the bequest of the enlightened ones of the past: to arrive at the knowledge and insight of buddhahood without making an issue of meditation or effort. The body itself is Buddha—mind, Buddha, sentient beings, enlightenment, and affliction are different in name but one in essence. You should know that your own mind essence is in substance beyond annihilation and eternity; its nature is neither defiled nor pure. Profoundly still, complete, it is equal in ordinary people and in saints. It functions freely, apart from mentation, intellection, and cognition: all realms of being are just mind revealing itself—how could there be any real origination or destruction of mere reflections? If you can realize this, you will be complete." If he had not had an independent view that dissolved the universe, he could not have spoken thus. Having attained realization at a blow and succeeding in seeing clearly, he ranked as one of the Zen masters.

Your spiritual nature cannot be separate from his—how could your basic mind possibly not have common ground? The existence of states of happiness and misery, superior and inferior conditions, depends solely on whether or not one has developed determination, whether or not one has met an enlightened teacher.

How can we see this story?

All at once he raises infinity—
Never has he clung to anything beyond him.

37

Yaoshan

Yaoshan called on Zen master Shitou and asked, "I know something about the canonical teachings of Buddhism, but I have heard that in Zen they point directly to the human mind to see its essence and realize buddhahood. I really don't understand this and beg you to be so compassionate as to teach me."

Shitou said, "Being just so won't do, not being so won't do either —being just so or not being just so won't do at all. What about you?" Yaoshan was at a loss. Shitou said, "Your affinity is not here. Go to Great Master Mazu's place for a while."

Following these instructions, Yaoshan went to visit Zen master Mazu and set forth the same question. Mazu said, "Sometimes I make 'him' raise his eyebrows and blink his eyes, sometimes I don't make 'him' raise his eyebrows and blink his eyes. Sometimes raising the eyebrows and blinking the eyes is right, sometimes raising the eyebrows and blinking the eyes is not right. What about you?"

At these words Yaoshan was greatly enlightened. He immediately bowed. Mazu said, "What truth have you seen that you bow?" Yaoshan said, "When I was with Shitou, I was like a mosquito climbing up an iron ox." Mazu said, "You have realized the truth; guard it well. Your teacher, however, is Shitou."

Yaoshan became a monk when he was seventeen years old. He learned many scriptures and treatises, and kept the monastic precepts strictly. One day he lamented to himself, "A real man should purify himself without laws. Why should one fuss over petty details of manner?" So he turned to Zen study. He first called on Shitou, then went to Mazu, with whom he became enlightened.

Yaoshan attended Mazu for three years. One day Mazu asked him, "How do you see things these days?" Yaoshan said, "Having shed my skin completely, there is only one true reality." Mazu said, "Your realization may truly be said to accord with the essence of mind and has permeated your whole body. Since you have come to such a realization, you should gird your loins and live on a mountain, wherever may be fitting."

Yaoshan said, "Who am I to presume to live on a mountain?" Mazu said, "Otherwise, there is no constant going without stopping, no constant staying without going. You may want to help yet there will be no help, and though you try to act there will be nothing done. You should make a boat—don't stay here." So Yaoshan left Mazu and went back to Shitou.

One day as Yaoshan was sitting, Shitou asked him, "What are you doing here?" Yaoshan said, "I'm not doing anything at all." Shitou said, "Then you're sitting idly." Yaoshan said, "If I were sitting idly, that would be doing something." Shitou said, "You said you're not doing—what aren't you doing?" Yaoshan said, "Even the sages don't know." Shitou praised him with a verse:

Though we've been living in the same place,
I do not know his name;
We go along with the flow of nature,
Being just so.
Even the eminent sages of old don't know him—
How could the careless rabble understand!

Later, when Shitou once said in a lecture, "Speech and activity miss the point," Yaoshan said, "Silence and inactivity also miss the point." Shitou said, "With me, not even a needle can enter." Yaoshan said, "With me, it's like planting flowers on a rock." Shitou approved of him. Later a group of disciples gathered around Yaoshan.

By this story it should be clear that the two schools of Qingyuan

(Shitou's teacher) and Nanyue (Mazu's teacher) are not different. They are really two horns of Huineng (teacher of both Qingyuan and Nanyue), who was a white ox on open ground, standing alone. Yaoshan studied with one and was enlightened with the other. There was no discrepancy at all.

At first Yaoshan asked Shitou, "I know something about the canonical teachings—what is the teaching of direct pointing to the human mind to see its nature and realize buddhahood?" To express this state, Shitou said, "Being so will not do, not being so will not do either—being so or not being so will not do at all." At this point there is no place to put self, and the other is not a matter in doubt: that is why Shitou explained in this way. But at this stage Yaoshan still clung to the ungraspable, and therefore he didn't yet know the import of the words. He stopped and thought for a while. Then Shitou directed him to Mazu to have him explain instead.

Because Mazu understood the heart of the matter, he said in behalf of Shitou, "I make 'him' raise his eyebrows and blink, or I don't make 'him' raise his eyebrows and blink. Sometimes it's right, sometimes it's not right." Mazu showed him how it differs according to the time. Then Yaoshan awakened to this point and knew that it all exists—seeing, hearing, discernment, knowledge, movement and action, going and coming. He then bowed. Mazu said, "What truth have you seen that you bow?" He said, "At Shitou's place I was like a mosquito climbing an iron ox." There was no place to bite into—his opinions and views ended, his intellectual understanding dropped off. Though he did not know it himself, he was a true human being.

Later Mazu asked him, "How is your view these days?" Knowing there is not a single mote of dust here, not the slightest flaw, he said, "Having shed my skin completely, only one true reality exists." It is exceedingly hard to reach this realm in Zen study. That is why Mazu praised him, saying, "Your realization can truly be said to accord with the mind essence and to permeate your whole body." He reached everywhere and comprehended everything. And though his experiences and activities were varied and changing up until the time he could say he wasn't doing anything at all, he realized it was all like planting flowers on a rock, with no traces at all.

As he questioned and sought the direct pointing to the human mind at first, he was greatly enlightened when the one who raises the eyebrows and blinks the eyes was pointed out to him. When he preached for people himself, he said, "I am speaking these words to you to reveal that which has no words. The original face of that one has no such features as eyes or ears." Because his virtue in the beginning and the middle was genuine, so in his final virtue he showed truthfulness and helped others.

So seekers of truth should study like Yaoshan. Although the Zen founders were not superior or inferior to each other in their virtues, Yaoshan was especially lofty in his dealings with students and austere with himself; so he had fewer than twenty students. The fact that he did not have many students was because of his austerity; it was because people couldn't stand hunger and cold. But there were many enlightened monks and laymen in his group.

Thus as seekers you should consider thorough study of prime importance and should not worry about abundance or scarcity of worldly things. It was thus that several of Yaoshan's students, with the same determination, spent forty years without lying down. Unless it is a congregation where there is enlightenment, there are no monks like that. You Zen students should hope to be brothers of Yaoshan's students of old, and determine to study to the point that his teachers reached.

Don't you see—that which causes the eyebrows to raise and the eyes to blink is right and not right. That state is not to be doubted—everyone has it. When you try to know it, you find it has no features such as ears or eyes. Therefore it cannot be discerned in seeing or hearing. It does not act at all. Furthermore, although it is something whose name you don't know even though it has always been living with you, yet it naturally comes along with you. Not only that, it causes you to be born, causes you to die, causes you to move and act, causes you to perceive and feel. It is what we call *This*.

You cannot find the truth outside yourself—how can you hope to see your true nature some other time? All the canonical teachings point to this truth. All beings are sustained by this, without end. Why seek proof elsewhere? Are you not raising your eyebrows and blinking your eyes right now? If you just see the one who perceives and feels, you won't doubt what the Zen masters say.

Now how can I add an explanation to this principle?

That one who is always lively—
We call the one raising the eyebrows, blinking the eyes.

38

Yunyan

Yunyan first studied with Baizhang for twenty years, then went to study with Yaoshan. Yaoshan asked him, "What else does Baizhang teach?" Yunyan said, "Once when he went up in the hall to lecture and the assembly was standing there, he dispersed them with his staff. Then he called to them, and when they turned their heads he said, 'What is it?'" Yaoshan said, "Why didn't you say so before! Today, through you, I have been able to see brother Baizhang." At these words Yunyan was greatly enlightened.

Yunyan became a monk when he was young and studied with Zen master Baizhang for twenty years without success. After that he called on Yaoshan. Yaoshan asked him where he had come from, and Yunyan replied that he had come from Baizhang. Yaoshan asked, "What does Baizhang say to the students?" Yunyan said, "He often says, 'I have a saying that contains all flavors.'" Yaoshan said, "Salt is salty, water is plain. What is neither salty nor plain is the constant flavor. What is the saying that contains all flavors?" Yunyan had no reply. Yaoshan said, "What can you do about the birth and death before your eyes?" Yunyan said, "There is no birth and death before my eyes." Yaoshan said, "How long were you with Baizhang?" Yunyan said, "Twenty years." Yaoshan said, "Twenty years with Baizhang, and your mundanity is still not gone."

Another day, as Yunyan was standing in attendance on Yaoshan, the Zen master asked him, "What other teachings does Baizhang expound?" Yunyan said, "Sometimes he says, 'Understand beyond all formulations and propositions.' " Yaoshan said, "Three thousand miles away, there's no connection." He also asked, "What else does he teach?" And Yunyan related the anecdote quoted in the opening story.

Now the basic point of Zen study is to clarify the mind and awaken to reality. So even though Yunyan studied with Baizhang for twenty years, since conditions weren't right he didn't realize enlightenment. After that he called on Yaoshan. So you shouldn't think that long study is necessarily good—only enlightenment of the mind is fundamental. And the meeting of right circumstances doesn't depend on whether one is a novice or experienced—preexisting conditions are what cause it to be so. It is not that Baizhang wasn't an enlightened teacher, it is simply that Yunyan didn't meet the right conditions.

Being a teacher is not merely a matter of gathering a group and looking after people—it is to make people penetrate directly to the root source and realize the fundamental. That is why the ancients always used to ask people where they came from. Extensive travel was to test teachers, so they wanted to see where the students had come from. Also they would ask what students had come for—this is to clarify the shallowness or depth of their determination and to see how far their development extended.

So in this case too Yaoshan asked Yunyan where he had come from. Yunyan said he had come from Baizhang, to show he had not been merely visiting here and there and wandering over hill and dale. Yaoshan and Baizhang were both public teachers and outstanding representatives of the Qingyuan and Nanyue lineages, respectively. So it was that Yaoshan asked what Baizhang was saying to his students.

At this point, if Yunyan had been worth his salt he would have brought up what he himself had learned, but instead he just mentioned what he had heard, saying, "He often says, 'I have a saying that contains all flavors.' " That one saying contains everything—everything is complete in it. But can people hear that expression?

In order to discern carefully, Yaoshan said, "Salt is salty, water is plain. What is neither salty nor bland is the constant flavor. What is the saying that contains all flavors?" After all it was something Yun-yan had not comprehended; because he used his mortal ears to listen uselessly to a clam's explanation, he was at a loss and had no answer.

So Yaoshan asked him, "What can you do about the birth and death before your eyes?" This is truly the most important thing for students, whether beginners or old-timers. Impermanence is swift, the matter of birth and death is important. Even if you have set off on travels and are robed and shaven as a monk, if you do not clarify the great matter of birth and death and do not attain to the path of lib-eration, you won't know the secret within you. Therefore you will not get out of the cage of the world and cannot escape the net of birth and death. In such a case it would seem you bear the robes and imple-ments of a monk in vain.

So as Yaoshan questioned him in this way to settle the man and not allow him any idle time, Yunyan immediately answered, "There is no birth and death before my eyes," saying what came to mind. But if you reach the point where you yourself are at peace and accomplish the original purpose of your study, there should not be any such views.

Yaoshan said, "How long were you with Baizhang?" He was ask-ing how many years Yunyan had cultivated the Way. Yunyan said, "Twenty years." Actually even though this ancient had been practic-ing without an idle moment, at this point it seemed as if he had wasted twenty years. So Yaoshan said to him, "You were with Bai-zhang for twenty years and your mundanity still isn't gone."

Even if you understand there is no birth or death and see there is no self or others, such a view does not perceive your own original head: you have not "let go over a cliff." If you do not immediately return your self to emptiness, your mundanity will not be removed, you will not break through sentiments and get out of prison. Isn't that sad?

That is why Yaoshan repeatedly questioned Yunyan—to lead him to thorough certainty. Nevertheless, at this point Yunyan still hadn't realized it. Even if he had attained understanding beyond all the for-mulations and propositions, still a hammerhead without a hole does not make a guiding principle. Even if he had some experience of cutting off the byways of myriad distinctions, he still didn't see his own original light. As it is said, "Three thousand miles away, there is no connection." Yaoshan pointed out to him again that it appeared as if Yunyan's coming to see him had been useless.

At this point, Yunyan cited Baizhang's hall-leaving saying—"What is it?"—but still was concerning himself with another's sayings and did not arrive at his own realization. Yet even as he brought up this story, he brought up the pure unadulterated Zen Way. And that is why Yaoshan said, "Why didn't you say so! Today, through you, I've gotten to see brother Baizhang."

Now the meaning of Baizhang's dispersing the assembly is really liberation and independence. There is no need to bother to do anything else.

But if he just let it go at that, it seemed that they'd never realize anything, so in order to rouse them he called to them, "Hey, everybody!" When you hit the south, the north moves, so they turned their heads without thinking. Baizhang then said, "What is it?" Unfortunately, it seems no one in his group understood. But though no one there had anything to say, Yaoshan far away said, "Through you I have gotten to see brother Baizhang."

When one of the enlightened ancients said something of the enlightened state, other enlightened ones would say they had met. It was like "the same wind for a thousand miles"; it was like "not so much as a thread interposed." Thus Yunyan first studied with Baizhang, then went to Yaoshan, finally succeeding in understanding both with nothing separating teacher and apprentice.

If you realize this state, you will not only have no further doubt about your eternal real self. You will also see through and cut through all the Buddhas and Zen masters; you will meet Yaoshan and Baizhang and see eye to eye with Yunyan and Daowu.

How can we convey this principle?

Without moving, the solitary boat
sails ahead in the moonlight;
As you look around, the reeds on the ancient bank
have never moved.

39

Dongshan

Dongshan called on Zen master Yunyan and asked, "Who can hear the teaching of inanimate things?" Yunyan said, "It can be heard by the inanimate." Dongshan asked, "Do you hear it?" Yunyan said, "If I heard it, you wouldn't hear my teaching." Dongshan said, "If so, then I don't hear your teaching." Yunyan said, "If you don't even hear my teaching, how much less the teaching of the inanimate." Dongshan was greatly enlightened at this. He spoke a verse to Yunyan:

> Wondrous, wondrous!
> The teaching of the inanimate is inconceivable.
> If you listen with your ears you won't understand;
> When you hear the sound with your eyes, then you'll know.

Yunyan approved.

When Dongshan was a boy he followed a teacher and recited the Heart Wisdom Scripture. When he came to the point where it says, "There is no eye, no ear, no nose, no tongue, body, or mind," he suddenly felt his face with his hand and said, "I have eyes, ears, nose, tongue, and so on—why does the scripture say they don't exist?" The tutor was amazed and said, "I am not your teacher." Then he directed Dongshan to a Zen master, who initiated him. He was fully ordained as a monk when he was twenty-one.

Dongshan was his mother's favorite son. His elder brother had passed away, his younger brother was poor, and his father had died. But once he aspired to the school of emptiness, he left his old mother and vowed he would never go back to his native place to see his relatives without having realized the Way. He left home with this determination.

Eventually Dongshan completed his study successfully. His mother, separated from her son, had no other support; day after day she looked for him, eventually becoming an itinerant beggar. When she heard where her son was living, she wanted to go see him, but Dongshan refused—he barred his door and wouldn't let her in because he wasn't willing to see her. Because of this his mother finally died of grief outside his room.

After his mother had died, Dongshan went out and took the rice she had had with her and mixed it in with the community's morning gruel as a funerary offering. Before long his mother appeared to him in a dream and said, "Because you kept your determination firm and would not see me, the delusive feelings of emotional attachment were ended on the spot; due to the power of that virtue, I have been born in the heaven of satisfaction."

Although the Zen masters were not better or worse than each other in terms of virtue, Dongshan, ancestor of our school, especially caused Zen to flourish. This was due to this power of leaving his parents and keeping his determination.

In the beginning of his Zen study, Dongshan joined the congregation of Nanquan. He happened to be there on the anniversary of the death of Nanquan's teacher Mazu. As they were preparing a commemorative ceremony, Nanquan asked the group, "We are having a ceremony for Mazu tomorrow—do you think he will come?" When nobody answered, Dongshan came forward and said, "He'll come when he has a companion." Nanquan said, "Although this is a young man, he is suitable for polishing." Dongshan said, "Don't demean the good or enslave the free."

Next Dongshan called on Guishan and said, "Recently I heard that National Teacher Zhong of Nanyang had a saying about the teaching of inanimate things; I don't understand the subtle meaning."

Guishan said, "Do you remember it?" Dongshan said that he did. When Guishan asked him to repeat it, Dongshan recounted the following story.

A monk asked the teacher, "What is the mind of the ancient Buddhas?" The teacher said, "Fences, walls, tiles, pebbles." The monk said, "Aren't those inanimate things?" The teacher said they were. The monk said, "Can they teach?" The teacher said, "They are always teaching, clearly, unceasingly." The monk said, "Why can't I hear them?" The teacher said, "You yourself don't hear, but you shouldn't hinder that which does hear." The monk said, "Who can hear it?" The teacher said, "The saints can." The monk said, "Do you hear it?" The teacher said, "No." The monk said, "If you don't hear it, how do you know inanimate things can teach?" The teacher said, "It's lucky I don't hear it, for if I did I'd be equal to the saints and you wouldn't hear my teaching." The monk said, "Then sentient beings have no part in it?" The teacher said, "I teach sentient beings, not the saints." The monk said, "After sentient beings hear it, then what?" The teacher said, "Then they are not sentient beings." The monk said, "What scripture is the 'teaching of the inanimate' based on?" The teacher said, "Obviously 'words that do not accord with the classics are not the talk of a scholar.' Haven't you read where the Flower Ornament Scripture says, 'Lands teach, beings teach, all things in all times teach'?"

After Dongshan had recited this story, Guishan said, "I also have it here, but I hardly ever meet anyone suitable for it." Dongshan said, "I don't understand—please teach me." Guishan stood his whisk up and said, "Understand?" Dongshan said, "I don't." Guishan said, "Words will never explain it to you."

Then Dongshan asked, "Is there anyone who sought the Way at the same time as you?" Guishan directed him to Yunyan. Dongshan asked, "What is this man like?" Guishan said, "He once asked me what a student should do in order to serve the master. I told him that one must simply cut off attachments. He asked if he would then be able to avoid violating my teaching, and I told him first of all not to say I am here."

Finally Dongshan left Guishan and went to Yunyan. Bringing up the preceding events, he asked, "Who can hear the teaching of the inanimate?" Yunyan said, "The inanimate can hear it." Dongshan asked, "Why don't I hear it?" Yunyan raised his whisk and said, "Do you hear?" Dongshan said, "No." Yunyan said, "If you don't even hear my teaching, how could you hear the teaching of the inanimate?" Dongshan said, "What scripture contains the 'teaching of the inanimate'?" Yunyan said, "Haven't you read where the Infinite Light Scripture says, 'Rivers, birds, trees and groves, all invoke the Buddha and the Teaching'?" At this Dongshan had an awakening.

After expressing his understanding, Dongshan said to Yunyan, "I still have residual habits that have not yet been exhausted." Yunyan said, "What have you done?" Dongshan said, "I don't even practice the holy truths." Yunyan said, "Are you happy?" Dongshan said, "Yes—it is as though I have found a jewel in a trash heap."

Dongshan also asked Yunyan, "What should I do when I want to see my true being?" Yunyan said, "Ask the messenger within." Dongshan said, "I'm asking now." Yunyan said, "What does he tell you?"

When Dongshan took leave of Yunyan, he asked, "After your death, if someone asks me if I can describe your reality, how should I answer?" Yunyan remained silent for a while, then said, "Just *this* is it." Dongshan sank into thought. Yunyan said, "You should be most thoroughgoing in your understanding of this matter."

Dongshan still had some doubts, but later he was greatly enlightened when he saw his reflection in the water as he crossed a river. Then he understood the meaning of what had gone before. He said in verse,

Don't seek from others
Or you'll be estranged from yourself.
I now go on alone—
Everywhere I encounter It.
It now is me, I now am not It.
One must understand in this way
To merge with being as is.

Dongshan's life study was now accomplished, and he was free from lingering doubts; this was how it came about.

As for the story of the teaching of the inanimate, it began when a worker asked the national teacher of Nanyang, "I've heard that you say inanimate things teach. I don't understand this, and ask for your instruction." The teacher said, "If you would ask about the teaching of the inanimate, you should understand the inanimate—only then will you hear my teaching. Just ask after the teaching of the inanimate."

The worker said, "At the moment I'm just going by expedients for animate beings—what is the relation of inanimate beings?" The teacher said, "In all present activities, as long as the twin currents of 'profane' and 'holy' do not arise and vanish, this then is mystic consciousness that is not in the realm of being or nonbeing yet is fully perceptive and aware. It is just that it has no emotional consciousness or binding attachments. That is why the sixth founder of Zen said that the senses discerning objects is not consciousness."

This is how the national teacher spoke about the teaching of the inanimate. That is, he said that as long as profanity and holiness do not appear and disappear in the midst of activities, this is mystic consciousness that is not in the province of either existence or nonexistence, yet is fully aware. People usually think that "inanimate" means things like walls, pebbles, lamps, and pillars. This is not what the teacher is saying. He means there is a mystic consciousness in which the views of ordinariness and holiness are not divided, emotional attachments to illusion and enlightenment are not produced—it is not conceivable by emotional assessments and discrimination, it is not the movements of birth and death, coming and going. This mystic consciousness is fully perceptive and aware, but it is not sentimental or cognitive clinging.

Therefore Dongshan said that one must understand this way in order to merge with being as is. If you know that wherever you are you go on alone, you will never be apart from being as is. That is why an ancient said, "There is no knowledge outside of suchness that is proved by suchness, no suchness outside of knowledge that is cultivated by knowledge."

Suchness, being as is, is immutable, clear constant knowledge. Therefore it is said, "Round and clear, knowledge does not depend on thought." Full awareness is not attachment. Guishan said, "Words cannot explain it." Nanyang also said, "If sentient beings hear it, then they are not sentient beings." Thus having received the guidance of several teachers, since he understood true "insentience," Dongshan became the ancestor of a school and caused Zen to flourish.

Thus, observing carefully, you become fully aware of this mystic consciousness, which is called "inanimate" or "insentient." It is called inanimate because there is no running after sound and form, no bondage of emotion or discrimination. Nanyang really explained this principle in detail, so when you hear talk of the inanimate, don't make the mistake of understanding it as like fences or walls. As long as your feelings and thoughts are not deluded and attached, and your perception is not scattered here and there at random, then that mystic consciousness will be bright and unclouded, clearly aware.

If you try to grasp this, you cannot get it; it has no form, so it is not existent. If you try to get rid of it, you cannot separate from it; because it is forever with you, it is not nonexistent. It is not cognition or thought, it is not tied to any physical or psychological elements.

This is why Zen master Hongzhi said, "There is a wisdom apart from intellectual assessment and discrimination; there is a body which is not clusters of elements." In other words, it is this mystic consciousness. "Always teaching clearly" means it is always manifest—this is called teaching. It has one raise the eyebrows and blink the eyes, it makes one walk, stand, sit, and recline. Rushing, hurrying, dying here, being born there, eating when hungry, sleeping when tired—all is "teaching." Speaking, working, all activities are also "teaching."

It is not just spoken or unspoken teaching; there is something that appears obviously and is clearly never hidden. Everything, down to the chirping of insects, is revealed. Therefore everything is always teaching, clearly, unceasingly. If you can discern minutely, someday you'll be able to be a model for others, as was our ancestor Dongshan.

Now how can we explain this principle?

Extremely subtle, mystic consciousness is not mental
   attachment:
All the time it causes *that* to teach profusely.

40

Yunju

Yunju studied with Zen master Dongshan. Dongshan asked him, "What is your name?" Yunju said, "Daoying." Dongshan said, "Speak on the transcendental plane." Yunju said, "Speaking on the transcendental plane, I am not named Daoying." Dongshan said, "This is no different from the reply I made when I was with Yunyan."

Yunju left home to become a monk when he was still a boy. He was fully ordained at the age of twenty-five. His teacher had him study the texts of elementary individualistic Buddhism, but this was not to his liking, so he quit and went traveling. He went to the Zen master Cuiwei to ask about the Way, and there he heard from a traveler of the teaching of Dongshan. Eventually he went to Dongshan.

Dongshan asked Yunju, "Where have you come from?" Yunju said, "From Cuiwei." Dongshan said, "What words of instruction does Cuiwei have for his students?" Yunju said, "When Cuiwei was making ceremonial offerings to the image of a saint, I asked, 'You provide offerings for the saint, but will the saint come?' Cuiwei said, 'What do you eat every day?'" Dongshan said, "Did this conversation really take place?" Yunju said that it had. Dongshan said, "You didn't meet that adept in vain." Then he asked Yunju his name, and there ensued the dialogue cited at the beginning of this story.

Yunju realized the Way upon seeing the Dong River, and then spoke to Dongshan of his enlightenment. Dongshan said, "My way will spread endlessly through you." And once Dongshan asked Yunju, "I hear that Great Master Si was born in Japan and became a king—is it so?" Yunju said, "Great Master Si wouldn't even become a Buddha, much less a king." Dongshan agreed.

One day Dongshan asked, "Where have you been?" Yunju said, "I've been walking in the mountains." Dongshan said, "Which mountain is suitable to live on?" Yunju said, "Which is not?" Dongshan said, "If so, the whole country has been occupied by you." Yunju said, "No." Dongshan said, "Then you have found a road of entry?" Yunju said, "There's no road." Dongshan said, "How can you meet me if there is no road?" Yunju said, "Were there a road, I'd be a life apart from you." Dongshan said, "Hereafter even a thousand people, even ten thousand people, will be unable to hold this man back."

Once as Yunju was crossing a river along with Dongshan, the latter asked, "Is the water deep or shallow?" Yunju said, "Not wet." Dongshan said, "Coarse man." Yunju said, "Please, *you* say." Dongshan said, "Not dry."

Dongshan also said to Yunju, "Zen master Nanquan asked a monk, 'What scripture do you lecture on?' The monk said, 'The scripture on the incarnation of Maitreya, the future Buddha.' Nanquan said, 'When will Maitreya be incarnated?' The monk said, 'Now he is in heaven, in the future he will be born on earth.' Nanquan said, 'There is no Maitreya in heaven or on earth.'" Now Yunju asked Dongshan, "If there is no Maitreya in heaven or on earth, to whom is the name given?" Dongshan's seat rocked when he heard this. He said, "When I was with Yunyan, I asked a question that rocked the hearth—now that I have been asked this question by you, my whole body is running with sweat."

Dongshan and Yunju never differed in these dialogues. No one in Dongshan's congregation could equal Yunju.

Later Yunju built a hut on the mountain peak and didn't come to the monastery for ten days at a time. Dongshan asked him, "Why don't you come to meals?" Yunju said, "Every day a celestial spirit sends an offering." Dongshan said, "I thought you were an enlightened man, but I see you still entertain such views. Come tonight."

That night Yunju went to see Dongshan. Dongshan said, "O Hermit!" Yunju said, "Yes?" Dongshan said, "Not thinking good, not thinking bad, what is this?" Yunju returned to his hut and sat in absolute silence; hence the celestial spirit couldn't find him. After three days like this, the spirit vanished.

Once Dongshan asked Yunju, "What are you doing?" Yunju said, "Making bean paste." Dongshan said, "How much salt are you using?" Yunju said, "As needed." Dongshan said, "How is the taste?" Yunju said, "All right."

Dongshan said, "An incorrigible commits inhuman crimes—where is the caring?" Yunju said, "This is real caring."

After this Dongshan gave his approval and made Yunju leader of the students permitted personal interviews. When Yunju became a teacher in his own right, his teaching didn't flourish at first, but after he moved to Yunju great numbers of mendicants and lay seekers gathered there.

After Yunju saw Cuiwei, he studied with Dongshan and was a brother of Caoshan. Through the foregoing dialogues, the settling of doubt between teacher and apprentice was accomplished. Dongshan predicted that his way would spread limitlessly through Yunju, and those words were not in vain, as it was handed on through the generations, down to the present day. This way is now active; it has been handed down through the school of purity. The source has not dried up; it is cool as autumn.

When Yunju asked a single question, he set his great ability in action. Dongshan was not only shaken thereby, he even broke out in a sweat. This is a rare occurrence. But when Yunju was living in seclusion and a celestial spirit sent him food, Dongshan said to him, "I thought you were an enlightened man, but you still entertain such views." He told Yunju to come to him that night, and when he did, Dongshan called him by name, to which he responded. That which responded is that which should not receive celestial food. To settle the matter, Dongshan said, "Not thinking of good or bad, what is this?" When you completely arrive at this state and can see in this way, "the gods find no road to strew flowers on, demons and outsiders secretly spying cannot see you." At such a time even the Buddha's eye cannot see you. When he had realized this, he "made bean paste," putting in "what is needed." He was self-sufficient, relying on no one.

Therefore Yunju repeatedly committed the crimes of incorrigibles—"killing father and mother," "killing Buddhas and Zen masters," and so on. At this point there was no thought in his mind of "caring." Dongshan questioned him to test his insight: "Where is the feeling of parent and child?" Yunju said, "Only this is really the feeling of parent and child."

So when Yunju received the transmission as the foremost of the disciples, Dongshan purposely asked him, "What is your name?" When seeing someone in the meeting of teacher and apprentice, one doesn't go by former sense—this is why Dongshan asked Yunju what his name was. Of course Dongshan knew his name, but he still asked, not without reason. Yunju replied, "Daoying." Even if one goes on asking in thousands of different ways, it still must be *thus*. You shouldn't make up rationalizations.

Although he didn't disagree with Yunju's insight, Dongshan still wanted to see if he had the ability to pass through barriers and escape conventions, so he said, "Tell me again, on the transcendental plane." Yunju was already free from discriminatory consciousness, he was like a faceless man, a straw dog—so he said, "On the transcendental plane, I am not named Daoying." It is very difficult to reach this realm, but if you don't reach this stage in Zen study, you haven't the potential to be an adept. You will still be confused by intellectual complications. Because Yunju preserved this state carefully, in the end they had the dialogue about the great incorrigible. There was no discord.

If you can discern thoroughly, you will be true Zen practitioners who have done what is to be done. Now what can we say to see through this story?

Name or form it has never had—
What transcendence or immanence is there to speak of?

41

Daopi

Once Zen master Yunju said, "If you want to realize such a thing, you must be such a person; once you are such a person, why worry about such a thing?" Hearing this, Daopi was spontaneously enlightened.

It is not known where Daopi came from. He studied with Zen master Yunju, became his attendant, and spent years there. One time Yunju said in a lecture, "Zen Buddhists should have a reason when they speak. Don't be careless. What place is this? How can you take it easy? Whenever you ask about this matter, you should have some knowledge of right and wrong. . . . Above all, don't cling—if you cling, that's not it. . . . Someone who knows the truth will naturally know how to preserve it. Such a one is never hasty or careless—when he has something to say, nine times out of ten he remains silent. Why so? Because it may be of no benefit. Someone of thorough realization has a mind like a fan in winter, and cobwebs grow on his mouth because he hardly ever speaks out. This is not forced, it naturally happens so. If you want to attain such a thing, you must be such a person; once you are such a person, why worry about such a thing?"

Hearing how difficult it is to realize this matter, Daopi understood and finally finished with his life's concern. Later he became a teacher and richly expounded the Zen way of Yunju.

Once a monk asked, "How can one stop taking the reflection for the head?" Daopi said, "Who are you talking to about it?" The monk asked, "What should I do?" Daopi said, "If you seek from another, you'll be all the farther from it." The monk asked, "How about when I don't seek from another?" Daopi said, "Where is your head?" The monk asked, "What is the style of your school?" Daopi said, "The golden hen, embracing its young, returns to the blue sky; the jade rabbit, pregnant, enters the purple dusk." The monk asked, "When a guest comes, how do you treat him?" Daopi said, "The golden fruit is picked by monkeys early in the morning; jade flowers are brought by phoenixes at night."

Having first understood the true state through his teacher's indications, in expressing the style of his school Daopi said, "The golden hen (the sun) returns to the sky, the jade rabbit (the moon) enters the purple dusk." And when helping people, "Golden fruits are picked every day, jade flowers are brought every night."

Although there is no superiority or inferiority among stories for Zen study, you should thoroughly comprehend the ones just brought up. Why? If you want to attain such a thing, you must be such a person. Even if you can't find your head and come looking for it, it's still your head. As Dogen said, "Who says 'I'? It is 'I' who says 'who.'"

So when the professor Liangcui called on Mazu, Mazu shut the door when he saw him coming. Liangcui knocked on the door, and Mazu said, "Who is it?" Liangcui replied, "Liangcui," and as soon as he called out his name he was suddenly enlightened. He said, "Master, don't fool me. Had I not come to see you, I would probably have been cheated by the scriptures all my life." Mazu then opened the door and had him tell of his enlightenment. When Liangcui returned to his lecture hall, he dismissed his students, telling them, "What you know, I know; what I know, you don't know."

In truth, this realm "does not let the wind through." So when you penetrate thoroughly you find you have always been complete, never lacking. Even if you figure by means of thought, it is your self, no one else. Though you "shine alone," it is not discrimination. It too is yourself. It is not new.

That is to say, using your eyes, ears, mouth, hands, and feet, it is all your self. Fundamentally it is not to be grasped by the hand or seen by the eye; thus it is not a question of sound or form. It cannot be reached by ear or eye. When you comprehend thoroughly, you will know there is self. You will know there is oneself.

In order to know this, when you first put aside all affirmation and negation and don't depend on anything or get involved with others, then this mind alone is clear, brighter than the sun and moon. This mind is pure, purer than frost and snow. Thus it is not dark obscurity, being unaware of right and wrong; it is pure clarity, one's self spontaneously manifest.

So do not think that there is nothing apart from speech and silence, activity and stillness, nothing having no skin, flesh, bones, or marrow. And don't think it is a matter of being immobile, standing alone, not thinking of self or other, not minding anything, being like a stump, totally nonreliant on anything, being mindless as plants and trees. How can the study of the Buddha Way be the same as plants and trees? The view that there is originally no self or other, that there is nothing at all, is the same as the nihilistic view of outsiders, or the view of voidness held by those in the lesser vehicles of Buddhism. The ultimate principle of the great vehicle of Buddhism cannot be the same as the lesser vehicles or outsiders.

When you fully arrive and truly come to rest, it cannot be said to be a state of existence, because it is empty and clear; yet it cannot be called a state of nonexistence, because it is luminous and aware. This is not discerned by action, speech, or ideas, nor by mind, intellect, or consciousness.

How can we convey this principle?

With empty hands seeking on one's own,
Coming back with empty hands;
Where there is fundamentally no attainment,
After all one attains.

42

Tongan

Tongan studied with Zen master Daopi, whom he asked, "An ancient said, 'I don't care for what people of the world care for'—what do you care for?" Daopi said, "I have already gotten to be thus." Tongan was greatly enlightened on hearing these words.

Not much is known about Tongan, except that he studied with Zen master Daopi and had profound realization of Zen. When Daopi was about to die, he went into the teaching hall and said, "One of the Buddha's disciples stood out; what about the case of the Zen founder?" He said this three times, but no one responded. Finally Tongan came forth and said, "They stand in ranks outside the crystal curtain; for ten thousand miles there are songs of peace." Daopi said, "Only this ass could say that." After that Tongan became the teacher in the hall.

"One of Buddha's disciples stood out" refers to when Shakyamuni Buddha and Kasyapa first met, whereupon the truth was communicated. After that Kasyapa practiced austerities and later assisted Buddha in teaching. Although Kasyapa was not present at the meeting that took place at the time of the Buddha's death, all the followers were entrusted to Kasyapa. When Daopi was about to die, to reveal his successor he said, "What about the case of the Zen founder?" He said it three times but no one understood, so no one answered.

The polar mountain juts out immutable beyond all other mountains; the orb of the sun shines bright before myriad forms. There-fore "they stand in ranks outside the crystal curtain." Really there is nothing to compare to it. Because the whole being is independent, there is no second person. Thus there is not a mote of dust for ten thousand miles. Where are cunning ministers and fierce generals now? Singing hallelujah, everyone is at peace.

Tongan was an extraordinary Zen monk. In Zen study you must reach this state before you can succeed.

Such was his outstanding practical application and extraordinary attainment of Zen. He had revealed his excellent achievement ear-lier. This is why he said, " 'I don't care for what worldly people care for'—what do you care for?" "What people of the world care for" means that they love themselves and others. This care gradually in-creases. Then they care about their surroundings and subjective states. This care gets deeper and more attached. Adding fetters to bonds, they then care for Buddhas and Zen masters. In this way, at-tachment becomes more and more contaminated. Finally the causes of people's habitual actions become continuous; they are originally born from lack of freedom, and die in lack of freedom. This all just comes from attachment.

Therefore discrimination between sentient beings and Buddhas, between male and female, between animate and inanimate beings, is attachment to forms. You should get rid of this attachment right away. When there is no rule, no thing, and you don't discern what it is, so you are entirely unknowing and nondiscriminating, this is at-tachment to formlessness; so don't linger here.

Even when you're attached to forms, once you become inspired to transcend them you can naturally attain to truth. But if you grasp the view of formlessness and fall into the immaterial realm, unfor-tunately after eons have passed and your life in formless heaven ex-pires you will fall into uninterrupted hell. This is what is called mind-less annihilation of thought. Form and formlessness are both objects of attachment for worldly people. In the midst of forms you see yourself and others, while in formlessness you forget yourself and others. Both are wrong.

So Zen students should not have the attachments of worldly

people. First you should free yourselves from all erroneous views discriminating between right and wrong, good and bad, male and female. Then you should not dwell in nondoing, unconcerned, formless quiescence. If you want to realize this, don't seek from others, don't search outside yourself. You should look into the state before you were embodied—there will be no difference or distinctions.

But don't plunge into darkness, don't be as though in a ghost cave in a black mountain. This mind is originally wondrously bright and shining, not dark; this mind is clear and open, wholly luminous. Here there is no wearing of skin, flesh, bones, or marrow, no sense organs or objects, no delusion or enlightenment, no defilement or purity.

The Buddha has not preached anything for you, and there is nothing for you to ask a teacher. Not only have sound and form not been distinguished, there are not even any ears or eyes. And yet the mind-moon shines round and bright; the eye-blossom blooms, its pattern fresh and clear. You should go all the way to reach this realization.

How can you understand this principle? I'll add a saying in your behalf—quickly set your eyes before being:

The mind-moon and eye-blossom have fine bright color—
Opening beyond time, who is there to enjoy them?

43

Liangshan

Liangshan studied with Zen master Tongan, who asked him, "What is the business under the patchwork robe?" Liangshan had no answer. Tongan said, "In studying Buddhism, if you don't reach this state, that is most miserable. You ask me and I'll tell you." Liangshan said, "What is the business under the patchwork robe?" Tongan said, "It is within." Liangshan was thereupon greatly enlightened.

It is not known where Liangshan was from. He studied with Tongan and served as a personal attendant for four years, taking care of his robes and bowl. One time as Tongan was going up into the hall for the morning congregation, at which it is usual to wear the patchwork robe, Liangshan brought the robe for Tongan. As Tongan took the robe he asked, "What is the business under the patchwork robe?" Liangshan couldn't answer; when Tongan answered for him, he was greatly enlightened. Liangshan prostrated himself, so moved that his tears wet his robe. Tongan said, "Now that you are awakened, can you answer?" Liangshan said he could. Tongan said, "What is the business under the patchwork robe?" Liangshan said, "It is within." Tongan said, "Inner being—it exists within."

After that Liangshan often spoke of inner being in his teaching, and after he became an abbot many people asked him about "the business under the patchwork robe." Once when a student posed this question, he said, "Even the saints don't reveal it."

Another time a student asked, "When it is impossible to guard the home against thieves, then what?" Liangshan said, "If you recognize them, they won't be enemies." The student asked, "How about after recognizing them?" Liangshan said, "You'll exile them to the land of nonorigination." The student said, "Isn't that where they settle and live?" Liangshan said, "Stagnant water doesn't hide a dragon." The student asked, "What is the dragon in living water?" Liangshan said, "It makes waves without making a ripple." The student said, "How about when the waters are emptied and the mountains leveled?" The master got down from his seat, grabbed the student, and said, "Don't wet the corner of my robe."

Once a student asked, "What is the student's self?" Liangshan said, "In the heartland, the emperor; beyond the borders, the general." In this way, whenever he taught people he presented inner being to them.

In the story mentioned first, Zen master Tongan said, "In learning buddhahood, if you don't reach this state, that is most miserable." How true are these words! Even if you sit still until your seat breaks through, even if you persevere mindless of fatigue and even if you are a person of lofty deeds and pure behavior, if you haven't reached this realm you still can't get out of the prison of the world. Even if you are extremely eloquent and skillful in preaching, if you haven't reached this state the king of death has no fear of your words. Even if you are trained for many years and your thoughts are ended and your feelings are settled, your body like a dead tree and your heart like cold ashes, your mind never stirring in the face of events, even if you finally die sitting or standing and seem to have attained freedom in life and death, still if you haven't reached this realm it is all of no use in the house of the enlightened ones. Therefore an ancient said, "The past adepts all considered this business to be the one matter of importance."

Once Zen master Liangshan asked a monk, "What thing in the world is most miserable?" The monk replied, "Hell is most miserable." Dongshan said, "No. What is most miserable is to wear this vestment and fail to clarify the great matter."

Dongshan's great disciple Yunju quoted this saying to his disciples and said, "My late teacher said that hell is not what is really miserable—to wear this vestment and yet not understand the great matter is what is really miserable. You should exert yourselves more. Don't weary of your journey for enlightenment, don't violate the ways of the Zen community. An ancient said, 'If you want to be able to carry this matter through, you must stand atop the highest mountain and walk on the bottom of the deepest sea—only then will you have some life.' If you haven't comprehended the great matter, for the time being you should walk the mystic path."

Furthermore, in the introductory chapter of the Lotus Scripture, about Shakyamuni and all the Buddhas, it says, "The Buddhas only appear in the world for the cause of one great matter. That is to reveal the knowledge and vision of buddhahood, and to enable people to realize and enter it."

Indeed, to clarify this one great cause is considered the great matter. There is nothing to be delighted about in just being a Buddhist initiate in form—if you do not understand this matter, after all you are no different from worldly people. Why? Because you are no different in seeing with your eyes and hearing with your ears; and it is not only in relating to outside objects—you cannot forget thoughts about objects either. In this case, even though you may have become a monk or a nun, it is only a change in appearance—ultimately you are no different from people of the world. After all when your breath stops and your eyes close, your spirit will be impelled by things and flow in the world; though it seems there is a difference in class between being born a while in the human world and in a celestial realm, cyclic change will continue indefinitely, like a wheel going round and round.

What is the original purpose of making people leave their worldly attachments and be free from passions? It is just to allow them to arrive at the knowledge and insight of buddhahood. The reason for taking the trouble to establish Zen communities and assemble ordained and lay people is just to reveal this matter. That is why the meditation hall is called the place for selecting Buddhas. The leader is called the guide: it is not a matter of arbitrarily gathering people and making a fuss; it is only for the purpose of making people understand themselves. Therefore, even if you are formally a monk and a member of a monastery, if you don't understand this matter you are just toiling without accomplishing anything.

Especially in this degenerate age, this sick society, even if new students try to train their bodies and minds according to the guidelines of past enlightened ones, if their characters are crooked and devious they cannot succeed in Zen study. Monks of recent times are not settled in their actions, and do not try to learn all the greater and lesser refinements of behavior as well as the inner and outer mental techniques. For this reason it is as though there were no monkhood.

Yet even if your behavior and mental training are like those of ancient times, if you don't clarify the basis of mind this training will only result in elevated human states and will be involved with attachment. Furthermore, if you don't clarify the basis of mind and your behavior is unruly too, you are receiving the offerings of the faithful in vain. People like this are all bound for hell.

Yet an ancient worthy said, "Society has declined and people are lazy, but even if your behavior and mental discipline are not like that of the ancient sages, if you carefully and thoroughly clarify the one great matter, perhaps you will be no different from the Buddhas in this. The Zen masters and past sages will be your siblings. Fundamentally there is no world to leave—are there indeed any realms of being through which to transmigrate?" So meditate carefully, study meticulously, and clarify the matter under the patchwork robe.

In this great matter, there is no separation between eras of truth, imitation, and dereliction; and the various countries are no different. So don't lament that it is a sick society where Buddhism is degenerate. Don't regret that you are people of a remote country. So far as this matter is concerned, even if a thousand Buddhas all came at once and tried to give it to you, even the power of the Buddhas wouldn't suffice.

Therefore this is not a path that can be handed on to one's children, not a path that can be received from one's parents. One can only practice it oneself, realize it oneself, and attain it oneself in one's own being. Even though there be countless ages of practice, self-realization happens in an instant. Once you are inspired, not even heaven and earth can be found. Once you reach this place, eternity is illumined—how could there be anything given by the Buddhas?

So if you want to fully arrive at this place, first you must give up everything. Don't even seek the realm of buddhahood or Zen mastery. How much less should you have any self-love or dislike of others! Without arousing any intellectualization, just see directly—there is definitely something that has no skin or flesh; its body is like space, with no particular form or color. It is like pure water, being clear through and through. Empty and clear, it is just a matter of being completely aware of it.

How can we reveal this principle?

The water is clear to the very depths;
It shines without needing polish.

44

Dayang

Dayang asked Zen master Liangshan, "What is the formless site of enlightenment?" Liangshan pointed to an icon of the Bodhisattva of Compassion and said, "This was painted by Mr. Wu." Dayang was about to say something, when Liangshan grabbed him and demanded, "This is the one with form—which is the formless one?" At these words Dayang attained enlightenment.

This dialogue took place when Dayang first called on Liangshan, after having studied the Scripture of Complete Enlightenment and subsequently gone on a study pilgrimage. Upon awakening, Dayang bowed and stood there; Liangshan asked him, "Why don't you say something?" Dayang said, "I don't refuse to speak, but I'm afraid it would get onto paper." Liangshan laughed and said, "These words will be inscribed on stone yet." Then Dayang presented a verse:

In the past, as a beginner, I studied Zen in error,
Traveling over myriad rivers and mountains seeking
　　knowledge.
Clarifying the present, comprehending the past,
After all it is hard to understand—
Even if you speak of no mind, there's even more doubt.
The teacher has pointed out the ancient mirror
In which I see reflected the time before my parents bore me.
Now having learned, what is attained?

Release a blackbird by night,
And it flies covered with snow.

Liangshan said, "The school of Dongshan will rest on you."

Dayang became famous all at once. When Liangshan died, he went to another monastery, where the abbot turned the leadership over to him. Thenceforth the school of Dongshan became popular, with many people coming to study this way.

Dayang had an extraordinary presence and was very dignified. Even from childhood he only ate once a day. As a monk, he took the bequest of the ancient worthies seriously and neither left the sanctuary nor lay down to sleep. He continued in this way even when he was over eighty years old. Finally he took leave of the community one day and died.

In truth, that which is to be considered most essential in Zen study is this "formless site of enlightenment." It has no shape or form, it bears no name. Though it therefore has nothing to do with words, nevertheless there is after all definitely a place that is clearly apparent. This is what is called the appearance before birth.

In order to show this realm, Liangshan pointed to an icon of the Bodhisattva of Compassion painted by a Mr. Wu. It was just like pointing to a mirror. This is what is known as "having eyes yet not seeing, having ears yet not hearing, having hands yet not grasping, having a mind yet not cognizing, having a nose yet not smelling, having a tongue yet not tasting, having legs yet not walking." It is as though the faculties were all useless, the whole body useless furniture. It is like being a wooden man, an iron man. At this time seeing form and hearing sound have been escaped.

As Dayang was about to say something further at this point, Liangshan, to prevent him from remaining pinned down, quickly grabbed him and said, "This is the one with form—which is the formless one?" By means of the unused, he made him aware of the faceless. It was like recognizing oneself by looking in a mirror.

In ancient times there was a mirror in which one could see all the internal organs of the body, each of the thousands of pores and hundreds of bones.

The point where you have eyes and ears but do not use them is where you see the realm where there is no body or mind. It is not only breaking through all forms; the darkness of mindless nondiscrimination is broken through, heaven and earth are not separated, myriad forms do not sprout up. This state is perfect and complete.

Actually it is not only that the school of Dongshan came to flourish all at once after Dayang reached this realization—in fact all the Zen masters saw in this way.

After Dayang had understood this essence, a monk asked him, "What is your family style?" Dayang said, "The full pitcher, though overturned, does not pour; there are no hungry people in the whole world." The reality of this state is such that you cannot expel it even though you overturn it, and it does not give way even though you push it. You cannot pick it up even though you pull at it, and no trace is left even though you touch it. Therefore it is not within reach of ear or eye. Though it comes along with speech and silence, action and stillness, it has never been obstructed by action or stillness. It is not only the Zen masters who have this thing—everyone in the world has it. That is why Dayang said there are no hungry people in all the world.

Now that you have encountered the way of the ancient Buddhas, investigate exhaustively and continuously, until you realize your self before you were born, before form and void came to be, reaching the point where there is no form or description at all, seeing where there is absolutely nothing outside, where you cannot grasp the elements of body or mind even if you grope forever. If you can realize the point where there's never been any lack, then you'll be a true descendant of the Zen masters.

Now how can we convey this principle?

The round mirror hung high, it clearly reflects all;
Colored paints in all their beauty cannot depict it completely.

45

Touzi

Touzi studied with Zen master Fushan, who told him to contemplate the story about the outsider who said to Buddha, "I do not ask about the spoken or the unspoken," to which the Buddha replied with silence. Touzi spent three years on this story, when one day Fushan asked him, "Do you remember the story? Try to quote it." As Touzi was about to reply, Fushan covered his mouth; Touzi was thereupon awakened.

Touzi was unusually sharp; he left home to enter a monastery when he was only seven years old. He took examinations in the scriptures and became ordained when he was fifteen. He studied Buddhist philosophy, but before long he lamented, "Three incalculable eons, said to be the time required for perfect enlightenment, is a long road to travel. Even if one wears oneself out, what benefit is there?"

So he went to the ancient capital and attended lectures on the Flower Ornament Scripture. The doctrines expressed there seemed like stringing pearls. Once when he read a certain set of verses in that scripture, coming to where it speaks of "the inherent nature of mind itself," he reflected deeply and said, "The truth is beyond written words—how can it be made the subject of a lecture?" So he gave up academic studies and began to visit Zen teaching centers.

At that time Zen master Fushan was an outstanding public teacher. One night he dreamed he was raising a green hawk, and took this to be an auspicious omen. The very next morning Touzi arrived, and Fushan politely welcomed him. Fushan had Touzi contemplate the story of the Hindu questioning Buddha, and Touzi finally became enlightened.

On awakening, he bowed to Fushan, who said, "Do you realize the mystic potential?" Touzi said, "Even if it exists, it too should be ejected." An attendant standing by at the time said, "Today Touzi is like a sick man who has finally broken out in a sweat." Touzi turned to him and said, "Shut up—if you rattle on, I'll puke."

Three years after this, Fushan brought out the teaching of the Dongshan lineage and taught it to Touzi, who accorded with it in every way. Fushan handed on to him the symbolic relics that he had received in trust from Dayang—a portrait of Dayang, a pair of leather shoes, and Dayang's ceremonial robe. Fushan told Touzi, "Continue the way of that school in my stead. Don't remain here for long. You should keep it well." Finally he wrote a verse to send him off:

The polar mountain stands in space,
Sun and moon around it.
Myriad peaks gradually approach it,
The white clouds are always changing.
The way of the Zen founder flourishes,
The screen over the cave of Zen is lifted.
A golden phoenix lodges in a dragon's nest;
The moss in the imperial garden is not to be trampled.

The Buddha's wheel of true teaching was communicated intimately from west to east; in China, five schools of Zen flourished, each one using different devices, so that the styles of the schools were somewhat different. There were phoenixes, there were dragons and elephants; they didn't group together, but none of them was inferior to another.

Touzi accorded with Dayang in word and deed, so he should be called a descendant of the Dongshan school. Zen master Fushan succeeded to Shexian, so he was a descendant of the Linji school. A phoenix is not to be lodged in a dragon's nest, so Fushan sent Touzi to master Yuantong Xiu.

When Touzi got to the assembly of Yuantong, he never called on the master or asked any questions; he just used to sleep a lot. One of the functionaries reported this to Yuantong, saying, "There is a monk in the hall who just sleeps every day. You should enforce the rules." Yuantong said, "Don't do anything yet; let me handle it."

Yuantong then took his staff and went into the hall, where he saw Touzi sleeping. He hit the seat and scolded him, "I have no extra rice here to give you so you can just eat and sleep." Touzi said, "What would you have me do?" Yuantong said, "Why don't you ask about Zen?" Touzi said, "Fine food is not for a satisfied man to eat." Yuantong said, "What about the fact that many people do not agree with you?" Touzi said, "What would be the use of waiting for them to agree?" Yuantong said, "Who have you seen?" Touzi said, "Fushan." Yuantong said, "I had marveled at such stubborn laziness," and they both laughed. Henceforth Touzi became famous.

This is what is recorded in the *Five Lamps Merged in the Source*. In the *Continued Record of Sayings of Ancient Adepts* it says, "Zen master Touzi got the teaching from Zen master Fushan. Fushan had spent time with the great teacher Dayang, and they were in complete accord. Dayang ultimately transmitted the teaching of his school to Fushan, and wanted to hand on his shoes and robe to Fushan, but Fushan refused, saying that he had already gotten the transmission from another teacher. When Dayang lamented that there was no one to transmit his branch of Zen, Fushan said, 'The style of the school of Dongshan has come to an end and will be difficult to revive. You are advanced in years, so if there is no one to transmit it, then I will keep the robe of faith and hand it on to another in your stead, so that this way will continue.' Dayang allowed this and said, 'I'll write a verse and leave it with you for you to use as a proof.' Then he wrote:

> The grass on Dayang Mountain
> Depends on you for its value to be great.
> Where unusual sprouts grow in profusion,
> Deep and dense, the spiritual roots are made firm.

In the end he said, 'The one who receives this teaching should remain hidden in the community for ten years before bringing it out.'"

Later Touzi and Fushan met, and Fushan entrusted him with the

teachings of the Dongshan school, giving him the portrait of Dayang, the robe of faith, and Dayang's verse. He said, "You inherit the
way of Dayang in my stead." Subsequently it actually turned out
that Touzi finally appeared in the world as Dayang's successor after
the passage of ten years. In Dayang's verse, the place "where unusual
sprouts grow in profusion" refers to Touzi, while "the value becoming great" refers to Fushan.

Just as had been foretold, Touzi finally appeared in the world as a
public teacher. Offering incense, he said, "Do you know where this
stick of incense comes from? It is not produced by sky and earth, it is
not made by yin and yang. Anterior to the prehistoric Buddhas, it
does not fall into any rank. Transmitted from the Burning Lamp
Buddha through the Seven Buddhas of antiquity, it finally came to
the Sixth Founder Huineng, and divided into seven streams in
China. In the year 1065 I personally received the transmission and
verse of the school from Zen master Fushan, being given thorough
confirmation of my understanding. He told me to continue the
teaching of Dayang in his stead. Although I didn't know Zen master
Dayang, in Fushan's teaching he was able to recognize who could
succeed to that way. So I don't dare be ungrateful to Fushan's bequest
and the mission he entrusted to me; I respectfully offer this incense to
the great master Dayang. Why? Because one's parents and the Buddhas are not dear—it is the truth that I consider dear."

Thenceforth Touzi expounded the Zen way of Dayang, and had
Zen master Furong Daokai as his successor.

Zen master Fushan was a seventh-generation successor of master
Linji and the direct successor of master Shexian. He had left home to
follow a Zen teacher while still a boy. A monk came for an interview
with that teacher and asked him about the story where an ancient
master said the living meaning of Zen was a cypress tree. Watching
the teacher press the monk with questions, Fushan became enlightened. Later he visited several teachers and reached accord with all of
them. He called on Zen masters Fenyang and Shexian, and received
the seal of approval from both of them; finally he became the heir of
Shexian. He also called on Dayang and reached accord with him too.

Thus when Dayang wanted to hand the teaching of his school

over to Fushan, Fushan declined, saying he already had attainment elsewhere. Because Dayang ultimately was left without any living successors, even though he didn't accept the transmission himself, Fushan was entrusted with it so that the transmission wouldn't be cut off. Later he found the appropriate person and secretly handed it on. At this point it should be realized that the lineages of Qingyuan and Nanyue are basically not separate.

In fact, Fushan transmitted the Zen teaching of Dayang in his stead because he lamented the fact that the whole school of Dayang was about to die out. But followers of our school say that the school of Nanyue is inferior to that of Qingyuan; while followers of the Rinzai school say that the teaching of Dongshan had died out and was helped by the Linji school. Both of these groups seem ignorant of the essence of Zen. Whether in our school or another school, if there is a true person no one in either school should doubt.

As for the story mentioned at the beginning of this chapter, a Hindu said to Buddha, "I don't ask about the spoken or the unspoken." Because it is the path that does not fall within the scope of speech or silence, the Buddha did not say anything. This is not concealing or revealing, it is not self or other, it has no inside or outside, no absolute or relative. As the Buddha indicated that it is like space, like the ocean, the Hindu suddenly understood. He bowed and said, "The Buddha, most kind and compassionate, has cleared away the clouds of my delusion and allowed me to enter truth." Then he left. Truly he had attained a state where he was like the clear sky without a fleck of cloud, like a still ocean without wind or waves.

But Buddha's disciple Ananda didn't know this, and asked the Buddha, "What did the Hindu realize, that he said he had gained entry?" Buddha said, "Like a good horse, he goes as soon as he sees even the shadow of the whip." This is truly the working of the enlightened teachers—in opening the treasury, not a single device is employed, not a word spoken, yet here awakening is realized, like reaching the right road upon seeing the shadow of the whip.

So do not stay in the realm of nonthought—see beyond this. Do not stay in the realm of inexplicability—clarify your mind further. Many people misunderstand the Buddha's silence. Some say, "With-

out a single thought being born, the whole being appears: it manifests alone, apart from words, like the mountains appearing when
the clouds are gone; one stands out relying on nothing, just like this."
If you compare this to former exercise of intellectual understanding
and outward seeking, it seems as if one has come to rest to some extent, but still skin and flesh are not yet shed and the cluster of consciousness is not yet gone.

If you want to unite with this realm, you must stop your breath
and cut off your deepest attachments to life, then look—what appears? Would you say it is nonthinking? Since it cannot be named or
identified, how could you say it is silence? It is not just the breath ceasing and the eyes closing—look at where the bones are scattered and
there is no trace of skin or flesh left: there is one thing that does not
belong to light or darkness, that is not male or female.

How can we convey this principle?

A steep mountain miles high—birds can hardly cross;
Who can walk on thin ice or the blade of a sword?

46

Daokai

Daokai studied with Zen master Touzi. He asked, "The sayings of the Buddhas and Zen masters are everyday affairs—is there anything else to help people?" Touzi said, "You tell me—do the emperor's commands in his own realm depend on the ancient kings?" As Daokai was about to speak, Touzi hit him with a whisk and said, "The minute you intended to come here, you already deserved a beating." Daokai was enlightened at this.

Daokai liked peace and quiet ever since youth, and secluded himself in the mountains. Later he went to the capital city and registered in a monastery. He passed the ordination exam in the Lotus Scripture and was ordained as a monk. He called on Zen master Touzi, and was ultimately enlightened. Upon awakening at the foregoing dialogue, he bowed and set off, but Touzi said, "Come here a minute!" Daokai didn't even look back. Touzi said, "Have you reached the realm where there is no doubt?" Daokai covered his ears.

Later Daokai became the chief cook in Touzi's community. Once Touzi said to him, "It is not easy to manage the affairs of the kitchen." Daokai said, "I don't presume so." Touzi said, "Do you boil the gruel, do you steam the rice?" Daokai said, "Helpers clean the rice and light the fire; workers boil the gruel and steam the rice." Touzi said, "What do you do?" Daokai said, "The teacher has kindly let him go free."

One day Daokai accompanied Touzi on a stroll in the garden. Touzi handed his staff to Daokai, who took it and went along. Touzi said, "In principle it should be thus." Daokai said, "It is not out of place to carry the teacher's shoes and staff." Touzi said, "There is still another one accompanying." Daokai said, "That person doesn't take orders." Touzi stopped.

That evening Touzi said to Daokai, "Our earlier talk is still unfinished." Daokai said, "Please say it." Touzi said, "The sun rises at dawn, the moon rises at dusk." Daokai then lit a lamp. Touzi said, "Your comings and goings are not in vain." Daokai said, "As long as I am with the teacher, in principle it should be thus." Touzi said, "In whose house are there no servants?" Daokai said, "You're old—you shouldn't be without them." Touzi said, "You are so thoughtful." Daokai said, "I am repaying my debt."

In this way Daokai thoroughly and meticulously clarified "that one experience." What about the meaning of his first question, "The sayings of the Buddhas and Zen masters are like everyday affairs—is there anything besides these to help people?" He meant, "Is there anything that the Buddha and Zen masters taught besides the present everyday activity?" It seems indeed as if he was presenting his understanding. But then Touzi said, "You tell me, do the commands of the emperor in his realm depend on the kings of old?" In truth, giving orders in the present does not depend on the authority of ancient kings. It is just that when one person is benevolent, myriad people naturally benefit from it.

In the same way, even if Shakyamuni Buddha were to appear in the world, and even if great master Bodhidharma were still alive, people shouldn't rely on their power—one can only attain enlightenment through one's own acceptance and personal realization. Therefore when you explain a principle and add flavor, this is still looking to another—you have not gotten free from intentional striving. That is why Touzi hit Daokai when he was going to speak further.

At this, to point out the fact of fundamental completeness that lacks nothing, Touzi said, "The minute you intended to come here you already deserved a beating." This is not a testimony of enlightenment. As soon as one begins to seek to find out what mind is, what Buddha is, one has already turned away from oneself and turned toward another. Even if you can say on your own that everything is revealed and naturally clear, and can talk of mind, nature, Zen, and the Way, none of this is free from striving. If there is any striving, there are clouds for ten thousand miles—you have already been long astray from yourself. Even if you were beaten for a thousand lives for myriad years, you could not escape from this mistake.

Therefore Daokai was enlightened at Touzi's words; he bowed and immediately set off, without even turning his head. As Touzi asked if he had reached the point where there is no doubt, what further doubtlessness was there to reach? To say there is would already be ten thousand miles from home. That is why as soon as the words of the Buddhas and Zen masters enter your ears, they have already defiled your ears. Even if you wash them for a thousand lives, ten thousand years, you cannot get them clean. That is why Daokai covered his ears and didn't let in a single word.

Because Daokai had seen this point completely, when he was the head cook he also said, "He is set free." "He" is not that which cooks rice, not the one who picks vegetables. Therefore carrying firewood and hauling water is all the activity of the worker and servant, ultimately not the part of the head cook. Though it seems as if the pot washer never rests twenty-four hours a day, ultimately he does nothing and touches nothing. Therefore Daokai said, "He is set free."

Even though Daokai had attained such insight, in order to ripen it Touzi handed him his staff when they went into the garden; Daokai took it and went along. Touzi said, "In principle it should be thus," letting him know that this is not something for the teacher to carry, that there is one who does not carry things. At this point Daokai saw through, so he said, "It is not out of place to carry the staff and shoes for the teacher."

At this, Touzi's "toes moved inside his shoes," and while he knew that Daokai had "taken up the staff," yet he had some suspicion that Daokai still had the understanding that any activity is not out of place, so he tested him again by saying, "There is still another accompanying." It is not merely not knowing the name in spite of having always lived together—it is an old geezer whose face is unknown; this is the one accompanying. Daokai had already seen this long before, so he said, "That person doesn't take orders."

Yet Daokai still had a shortcoming. Why? Because even if you know there is "that person" who does not accompany activity and is not involved or affected, if you only know it exists in this way there is still something doubtful. So at this point Touzi stopped without pursuing the principle to the end. That night he said to Daokai, "Our earlier talk was not conclusive." Then Daokai, in order to indicate that he already knew of the existence of the transcendent without doubt and thus had no shortcoming, said, "Please say it, teacher."

So then Touzi said, "The sun rises at dawn, the moon rises at dusk." The night air gone, the stars have moved, the moon is dim; the white clouds lie across the green mountain, not yet unveiling it. But this is yet a sun that rises unaccompanied, unique and alone. When the sun sinks below the mountains to the west, myriad forms are unseen; with no one coming or going, though the road is not distinguished still there is something that is not emptied. Therefore it gives rise to the moon.

In this realm, even though all becomes one, with no other thing mixed in, and you see no "other," there is a state that is of itself spiritually shining—its illumination breaks up all darkness. This is why Daokai lit a lamp. Truly he had fully arrived and clearly seen. Thus Touzi said to him, "Your comings and goings are not in vain." Having become familiar with this realm, twenty-four hours a day he had no idle time. Therefore he said, "While I'm with the teacher, it logically should be thus."

Although Daokai had perceived thoroughly, it seemed that he was understanding in terms of function, so Touzi, to test him again, said, "In whose house are there no servants?" Who has no servants? Daokai said, "You are old—you shouldn't be without them." There is one who is venerable and great and is never apart from oneself. That is why Daokai said to Touzi, "You are old and shouldn't be without them." Since Daokai perceived so thoroughly, Touzi said, "You are so thoughtful."

For ages and ages it has supported us, never leaving—we have been receiving the power of its grace for a long time. Even the polar mountain and the mountains that surround the world are not a fit comparison for the magnitude of this grace; even the oceans and continents are not a fit comparison for this virtue. Why? Because the mountains, sun, moon, oceans, and rivers all go on moving and changing with time, but the benevolence of this "old teacher" is ultimately not in the realm of becoming and decay. Therefore we are always receiving its grace. If we live and die in vain, never having once bowed to that venerable countenance, we will be eternally sunk in the sea of birth and death as disrespectful people. If we are diligent and careful, once we manage to see it, that great benevolence of myriad ages will be requited all at once. That is why Daokai said, "I am repaying my debt."

Having thus seen so completely, Daokai became a teacher himself. One day a student asked, "The tune of a foreign pipe does not fall within the range of the musical scale; its rhyme goes beyond the blue sky. Please play a song." Daokai said, "A wooden rooster crows at midnight, an iron phoenix cries at dawn." The student said, "If so, there is a one-phrase song in which the rhymes of a thousand ages are contained; all the students in the Zen hall recognize the tune." Daokai said, "A tongueless child can continue the harmony."

As he had matured thoroughly in this way, there were no "green mountains" blocking his eyes, no "clear stream" to wash his ears. So he looked upon fame and gain as putting rubbish in the eye; seeing form and hearing sound were to him like planting flowers on a rock.

Therefore Daokai never left the sanctuary, and vowed never to go to feasts. He didn't mind if people came, he didn't mind if they left; his community was of no fixed size. They had one bowl of gruel daily, and if there was not enough rice to make gruel, they would just have hot rice-water. The school of Dongshan flourished with his teaching.

Because his perception was intimate and his practical application was unerring, Daokai didn't forget the bequest of the sages of old. Even though he followed the teachings of the ancient Buddhas in this way, he still said, "I am ashamed to be a monastery abbot, inasmuch as there is nothing in my practice worth taking as an example. How can I sit here wasting the monastery supplies, abruptly forgetting the trust of the sages of yore? Now I am emulating the example of the ancient leaders. . . . Whenever I talk about the practices of the ancient sages, I feel there is nowhere to place myself. I am ashamed at how soft and weak the people of later times are."

Now, as his religious descendant nine generations later, I am immaturely preaching the way of the school; my actions are not worthy of being taken as examples or models by succeeding generations. My application of mind is not direct and straightforward. How can I presume to face three or five students and make up a saying or two? We should be ashamed—we should beware and be humble before the illuminating awareness of our spiritual ancestors and the hidden perceptions of the ancient sages.

Yet even so, you students are luckily descendants of Zen master Daokai, being the family of the school of Dogen. You should clearly discern the mind ground, concentrating carefully. With no thought whatever of fame or profit, without pride or conceit, stabilize your mental technique, tune your bearing precisely. Reach what you should reach, investigate what you should find out, take care of the task of your life's study; never forgetting the bequest of our spiritual ancestors, following in the footsteps of the sages of yore, look the ancient Buddhas in the eye. Even if this is a degenerate age, you should be able to "see a tiger in town." There may well be those who "find gold under their hats." This is my ultimate wish and hope.

Now how can I bring out the preceding story?

Even without rouge, ugliness cannot show—
Naturally lovely, the lustrous radiance and jade powder.

47

Danxia

Danxia asked Zen master Daokai, "What is the one statement that all the sages have handed on from time immemorial?" Daokai said, "If you call it a statement, you are in danger of burying the Way of Zen." At these words Danxia was greatly enlightened.

Danxia left home to become a monk at an early age. He became enlightened under the tutelage of Zen master Daokai. In his first inquiry he asked, "What is the one statement that all the sages since antiquity have handed on?" Although the successive enlightened ones have changed in appearance, there is always that which is handed on, which has no front or back, no above or below, no boundaries, no self or other. This is called the nonempty void. This is the true ultimate for all people; it is inherently complete in everyone.

Yet many students erroneously think of it as original nothingness, declaring that there is nothing further to say and nothing to know. The ancients called such people outsiders fallen into empty nothingness. They never become really free.

So you must be thoroughgoing and continue until all is exhausted and even emptiness is empty; yet there is still something that cannot be emptied. Investigating thoroughly, once you manage to see it, you will be able to make a statement. Therefore Danxia called it the statement that has been handed down.

At that time, Daokai pointed out to him, "If you call it a statement, you are in danger of burying the Way of Zen." Really this realm shouldn't be called a statement—this is a misnomer. It is like bird tracks in the snow; that is why it is said, "Where you hide there are no traces." Once perceiving and knowing have ceased, and skin, flesh, bones, and marrow are gone, what could be left as a trace? If you can succeed in not making any tracks at all, this will become manifest as a result. Yet when this realm is realized, it is called "communicating mind by mind." This is called the union of the ways of lord and minister; it is "subtle inclusion of both absolute and relative at once."

Now tell me, what do you think the form of this realm is?

The pure wind circling may shake the earth,
But who will pick it up and show it to you?

48

Wukong

Wukong studied with Zen master Danxia. Danxia asked him, "What is the self that is before the eon of emptiness?" As Wukong was about to reply, Danxia said, "You're still noisy—go away for a while." Then one day when Wukong climbed up to the mountain peak, he was greatly enlightened.

Wukong lectured on the Lotus Scripture when he was only eighteen years old. After being ordained as a Buddhist monk he went to western China and studied the scriptures and treatises, comprehending their great meaning. Then he left western China and went to study with Zen master Danxia.

After his sudden realization, Wukong came back from the mountain peak and stood by Danxia. Danxia slapped him and said, "I thought you knew it exists." Wukong joyfully paid his respects. The next day Danxia went up to lecture in the hall and said, "The sun illumines the solitary peak, green; the moon faces the valley stream, cold. The wondrous secret of the enlightened ones should not be placed in a little heart." Then he got down from the high seat. Wukong came directly forward and said, "Your lecture today can't fool me anymore." Danxia said, "Try to quote my lecture." Wukong was silent. Danxia said, "I thought you'd gotten a glimpse." Wukong then went out.

Later Wukong journeyed to the sacred mountain Wutai, and

thence to the capital. From there he went downriver to Changlu, where he called on Zen master Zuzhao. They reached accord as soon as they spoke to one another; Zuzhao had Wukong be his attendant, and made him assistant teacher after a year. Before very long Zuzhao retired due to illness and had Wukong succeed to the abbacy there at Changlu. Students came to him like rivers flowing into the ocean. Around the year 1130 he traveled to eastern China and became abbot of a famous monastery there. Subsequently he was appointed abbot at six great public monasteries.

Wukong was truly extraordinary, yet when he set his mind to Zen study he still worked especially hard. Thus when he was asked about the self before the empty eon he tried to reply. Danxia didn't approve, and sent him away for a while. Then one day he climbed the mountain peak and found "the ten directions without walls, the four quarters without gates." Having reached this point where the ten directions were right before his eyes, he attained understanding. Therefore he came back and stood by Danxia without saying a word. Danxia, realizing that Wukong knew "it exists," said, "I thought you knew it exists." Then Wukong joyfully paid his respects. Finally Danxia publicly acknowledged Wukong's enlightenment in a lecture.

Later when Wukong became a teacher he said, "At one slap from my teacher my cleverness was exhausted and I couldn't find any way to open my mouth. Is there anyone here who is always joyfully alive? If you would avoid biting a bit and carrying a burden, each of you settle yourself."

In truth, where enlightened people meet each other they walk in the realm before time and make manifest the scenery of the fundamental ground. If you haven't seen this realm, even if you sit silently for thousands of years, immobile as a dead tree, like cold ashes, what is the use?

And people often form a mistaken idea when they hear of the self before the empty eon—they think it means there is no self, no other, no before, no after, no birth or death, no sentient beings or Buddhas, that it cannot be called one or two, it cannot be understood as sameness or difference. Evaluating and thinking in these terms, they think as soon as you say a word you've already missed it, as soon as you give it a thought you immediately turn away from it; so they mistakenly stick to the state of a lifeless ghost and are like zombies.

Then again, some think it is not opposed to anything, so that one can call it mountains and be right, one can call it rivers and be right, one can call it self or other and be right. Others also say that mountains are not mountains and rivers are not rivers, it is just that "this is a mountain, this is a river." So they say; but what is the use? All of them have gone on false paths. Some are attached to forms, some have the same view as nihilists.

But this realm does not rest within the province of being or nothingness, so there is nowhere to stick your tongue in, nowhere to revolve your thoughts. And it doesn't rest on heaven and earth, or on before or after. Look and see where there is no place to tread under your feet—then you will have some realization of it.

Some say it nullifies guidelines and examples, some say it conveys not a breath; but these are both matters pertaining to intentional approach, and after all have turned away from the self. All the more so if you talk about it as the moon, the snow, the water, the wind—probably you all have cataracts in your eyes and are suffering from optical illusions.

What can you call "mountains"? Ultimately there is not a single thing to see. What can you feel as cool or warm? Ultimately there's not a single thing to give you. That is why you cling to things. If you sweep away both worldly phenomena and Buddhism all at once and then see, finally you will not doubt.

Don't look inside, don't seek outside. Don't try to quiet your thoughts or rest your body. Just know intimately; understanding intimately, cut off all at once, sit for a while and see. Though you may say there is no place in the four quarters to take a step and no place in the world to fit your body, ultimately you should not depend on the power of another.

When you see in this way, there are no skin, flesh, marrow, or bones set out for you; birth and death, coming and going, cannot change you. Having shed your skin completely, one true reality alone exists. It shines throughout all time, with no distinction of measure or time. Is this only to be called "before the empty eon"? This place is totally beyond distinctions of before and after.

If you want to know the reason why, it is because this realm is not affected by becoming, subsistence, decay, and annihilation. How can selfhood and otherness be considered causeless? When you have forgotten outside objects and abandoned conditioned thought within, and "even the clear sky gets a beating," you are clean and naked, bare and untrammeled. If you perceive minutely, you will be empty and spiritual, clear and sublime.

If you are not careful and thoroughgoing, you cannot reach this state. In reality, to clarify the issues of countless ages is a matter of an instant—with no feeling of hesitation, without producing intellectual interpretations, just see immediately and directly; then you will be free and independent.

So Zen students doing mental gymnastics are already proceeding wrongly. You should know you can never rest if you deviate even slightly. Meditate thoroughly and fully arrive. Without relying on others you will open up into enlightenment, vast and open as space.

Now tell me, how can we convey a bit of this principle?

The ancient stream, the cold spring—no one looks in;
It does not allow travelers to tell how deep it is.

49

Zongjue

Zongjue was an attendant of Zen master Wukong for a long time. One day Wukong asked him, "How is your view these days?" Zongjue said, "I must say it is 'thus'." Wukong said, "Not yet—speak again." Zongjue said, "How is what I said not right?" Wukong said, "I don't say that what you said is not right, but that you have not yet realized the transcendent." Zongjue said, "I can express the transcendent." Wukong said, "What is the transcendent?" Zongjue said, "Even if I can speak of the transcendent, I can't bring it out for you." Wukong said "Actually you cannot yet express it." Zongjue said, "You please say it." Wukong said, "You ask me and I'll tell you." Zongjue said, "What is the transcendent?" Wukong said, "I must say it is 'not thus'." Hearing this, Zongjue was enlightened; Wukong then confirmed his realization.

As Wukong's longtime attendant, Zongjue studied with him day and night, approaching Zen from every angle, never relaxing. When Wukong asked him one day how his view was and he said, "I should say it is 'thus,'" Wukong said, "Not yet—speak again." Actually he says now "it is thus," but there is something lacking. That is to say, although he knows how to be "thus," he doesn't know there is one that is "not thus."

Yet the whole of being was manifest to him, concealing nothing, so he wondered what could be lacking. He asked, "How am I not yet right?" People who understand like this may realize the state of "the green mountain towering alone after the white clouds have dispersed," but they don't yet know that there is a "mountain" even higher than this mountain. So Wukong said, "I don't say that what you said was wrong, just that you haven't penetrated the transcendent." Although all this study of his was the transcendental matter, he still had the fault of not knowing it exists. That is why Wukong said, "You still can't express it."

Still, speaking and thinking, even though one says "thus," one falls into the secondary and tertiary. He knew there is a place where nothing can be applied, and that is why he said, "Even if I can speak of the transcendent, I can't bring it out for you." He still didn't know his own self, and was still stuck in distinction and division. Therefore Wukong said, "You really can't say it." At that point his breath was ended, his strength exhausted. He asked, "What is the transcendent?" Wukong said, "I must say it is 'not thus'." This and the previous statement are further apart than sky and earth, than water and fire. Zongjue thought the whole thing was manifest to him, but Wukong didn't agree. Zongjue only said, "It is thus"—he was only like a solitary light shining clearly. But then he finally saw his mistake and came to realization, whereupon he received confirmation of his enlightenment.

Subsequently Zongjue became a teacher. A student asked him, "What is the Way?" He said, "Stop standing at the crossroads looking into the distance."

Once in a lecture he said, "Walk in the realm before time; free your body outside the world. Sublime realization cannot be reached by means of ideation; true enlightenment cannot be conveyed by words. Just being empty and serene, the spirit tranquil, the white clouds end at the cold cliff, the spiritual light breaks through the darkness, the bright moon follows the night-faring boat. At such a time, how can you act? Absolute and relative have never left the fundamental state; what has complete freedom to do with circumstances of speech?"

Really there are no bounds in empty tranquility; even if you talk about it you are not separated from it. To know the transcendent you must be like this. Still, to speak of "mind" and "essence" is not the transcendent at all. People also think that saying "mountains are mountains, rivers are rivers" is the transcendent, but this is mistaken. Dongshan said, "Only when you have realized that which transcends Buddha will you be able to speak at all." A student asked, "What is speech?" Dongshan said, "When it is spoken, you don't hear."

Zen master Banshan also said, "The unique road of transcendence has not been transmitted by the sages." And it is not "roaming freely according to one's nature," as you often say.

Another student asked Zen master Wukong, "What is the transcendent?" Wukong said, "The subtlety is before a single bubble has arisen—how could it admit the eyes of even the sages?" The "bubble" he refers to means the appearance of one's personal being. Before appearance is called the transcendental.

Therefore Zen master Gumu, another true heir of Daokai, said in a lecture, "When you know there is something transcending Buddha, then you can talk. Zen students, tell me—what is beyond Buddha? This person doesn't have the six senses or seven consciousnesses—he is an incorrigible, with no buddha nature. When he meets a Buddha he kills the Buddha, and when he meets a Zen master he kills the Zen master. Neither heaven nor hell can contain him. Do you know this one?" After a pause, he said, "Face to face, yet unaware—much slumber, excess sleep-talk."

In truth, when it comes to that which transcends Buddha, even Buddhas lose their lives, even Zen adepts are shattered: try to go to heaven, and heaven crumbles away; turn toward hell, and hell breaks apart. What place can you consider heaven, what place hell? What do you call myriad forms? All along there have been no traces or tracks. It's like when asleep—you don't even know yourself, so how could others discern? It is just clarity, with no such phenomenon as "enlightenment." These are indeed the words of an exalted master.

If you know the transcendent, the eye on your forehead will open, and at this time there will be some realization. But tell me, what is this principle like?

It's just like wedges above and below—
You can't push them in or pull them out.

50

Zhijian

One day in an address Zen master Zongjue quoted, "Buddha had a secret saying; Kasyapa didn't conceal it." Hearing this, Zhijian suddenly realized the mystic meaning. He wept as he stood there, unconsciously blurting out, "Why haven't we heard this before?" After the lecture, Zongjue summoned Zhijian and asked him why he had been weeping in the teaching hall. Zhijian said, "Buddha had a secret saying, but Kasyapa didn't conceal it." Zongjue gave him approval and said, "You must be the one Yunju predicted long ago."

Zhijian was a disciple of Zen master Zhenxie at Changlu monastery when Zongjue was the senior monk there. At that time Zongjue saw that Zhijian had the capacity for Zen. Later Zhijian went into seclusion in the mountains, and no wild beasts could bother him. He became enlightened in the middle of the night, and sought confirmation from Zen master Yanshou. Then he went back to see Zongjue, who by then was abbot at another monastery. Zongjue appointed him to the post of scribe. Then one day he quoted the aforementioned saying.

This saying comes from the Nirvana Scripture: "At that time Kasyapa said to Buddha, 'According to what you say, the Buddhas have secret sayings, but this is not true. Why? Because the Buddhas only have esoteric sayings, not a secret canon. Take, for example, the case of a magician's robot: though people see it move, they don't see what it is inside that makes it move. Buddha's teaching is different—it lets everybody see and know all. How can it be said that the Buddhas have a secret canon?' Buddha praised Kasyapa, saying, 'Very good. As you say, the Buddha has no secret canon. Why? Like the full moon appearing in the autumn sky, clear and unobscured, which everyone can see, so are the words of the Buddha—they are open and clear, pure and without obscurity. Ignorant people don't understand and say it is a secret reserve. The wise understand and do not call it a reserve.'"

This saying has long been used in Zen schools. Thus in this case too, Zhijian, hearing it quoted, became enlightened—truly it hides nothing. When you hear words, you should understand the heart of the matter—don't get stuck on the words. Saying "fire" is not fire, saying "water" is not water. That is why your mouth doesn't burn when you speak of fire and doesn't get wet when you speak of water. So we know that water and fire are in reality not words.

Zen master Shitou said, "When you hear words you should understand the source—don't set up rules on your own." Zen master Yaoshan said, "You should see for yourself. Don't eliminate words; I am using these words to reveal the unspoken for you. What originally has no ears or eyes?" Zen master Changqing said, "The ancestors of Zen all spoke of transmitting mind, not of transmitting words."

Great master Yunmen also said, "If this matter were in words, well, don't the canonical teachings contain words? Why would we speak of a special transmission outside of doctrine? If you go by learned understanding and intellectual knowledge, even the sages of the tenth stage, though they can expound the teaching like rain-giving clouds, still are criticized because their perception of essence is still like looking through gauze. Thus we know that all states of mind are far from reality. Even so, if you have realization, speaking of fire cannot burn your mouth; you can talk all day without anything sticking to your teeth and lips, and you will not have spoken a single word."

Therefore you should know that there is something that not only is speechless but doesn't even have a mouth. Indeed, not only has it

no mouth, it has no eyes either, no physical elements, no sense faculties—fundamentally there is not the slightest thing to it. Yet
though it is so, this is not void, it is not nothingness. It means that
even though you see things and hear sounds, it is not these eyes
seeing, not ears hearing. This is the way the faceless one is.

Your coming into being as a body-mind is the doing of this faceless one. Therefore this body-mind is not something created. If you
haven't reached here, you think it is the body arising from the relation of your father and mother, or that it is the body born of the results of actions. Therefore you think it is the body that comes from
sperm and ovum, that it is the body covered with skin and flesh. This
is all because you don't understand yourself.

Therefore, to let people know this realm teachers use unlimited
expedient methods to cause the senses to stop, making everything
cease. At this point, there is something that cannot be obliterated,
there is something that cannot be destroyed. When you get to know
this, it is not emptiness or existence, it is not light or dark. So it is impossible to say that one is deluded or enlightened. Therefore we can't
even call this realm buddhahood, and we can't call it truth, we can't
call it mind or nature. It is just a bright, clear light. So we can't call it
the light of fire or water—it is just empty, clear, and bright. Therefore though we try to look into it, it can't be seen through, and
though we try to grasp it, it can't be grasped. It is just clear awareness.

Therefore, when the three disasters of flood, fire, and gales arise
and the world is destroyed, this "thing" is not destroyed. When the
various realms and forms of existence come into being and myriad
forms and appearances are undeniably there, this "thing" does not
change. Therefore even the Buddhas can do nothing about it, nor can
the Zen masters.

If you want to reach this point, for the time being close your
eyes—where the breath ends and this body ends and there is no house
to protect you, all function is unnecessary, and you are like the blue
sky with no clouds, the ocean without waves—then you'll be somewhat in accord with it.

At this point, though there is nothing you can do, there is yet a
light: this light is not like the sun or moon—the whole sky is a moon,

so there is nothing to illumine; the whole world is a sun, so there is nowhere to shine. You should realize this thoroughly. If you cannot see this point, you will not only be confused by monks, nuns, men, and women, you will transmigrate through the various states of being in the worlds of desire, form, and formlessness. Even though you be Buddhist monks in form, you'll still be caught by the king of the underworld—won't that be shameful?

Buddhism fills the whole universe—there is nowhere it does not reach. If you try to reach it, how could you fail? This human body is not easily obtained; it is received due to the power of past virtues. If you once reach the point I have been describing, you will all be liberated. It is not male or female, not spirit or ghost, not ordinary or holy, not ordained or lay: there is no place to contain it, and when you try to see it your vision cannot reach it.

If you manage to arrive at this point, though you be a monk you are not a monk, and though you be a layman you are not a layman. You will not be confused or deluded by your senses, nor compelled by perception and consciousness. If you fail to arrive, you will go on being deluded and trapped by them. Isn't that too bad? If you can arrive at your fundamental completeness by effort, you should do so. Indeed, since people lack nothing, it is a pity that they wander so much in illusion once they have been deluded by their perception.

Just forget senses and objects, do not depend on mind or consciousness. Be diligent in this and you will surely arrive. But this is not gradual attainment; you must rouse yourself powerfully all at once to succeed. Without giving rise to partial understanding or interpretation, directly perceiving the fundamental source, you should thus reach it. Once you have arrived, you will be firmly grounded and unshakable.

An ancient said, "Studying the Way is like drilling for fire; don't stop when you see smoke." When you use all your strength at one stretch, you get fire. What stage does "seeing smoke" refer to? When you meet the skillful technique of an enlightened teacher and reach the stage where not a single thought is born, this is the time when you "see smoke." If you linger here and rest a while, this is like stopping at warmth; you should go on to see fire. This means to know that which is able to not produce a single thought. If you do not know your self, even though it may seem that you're at rest for the present, and though you may thus be like a dead tree, you are just a corpse whose spirit has not yet dissolved.

Therefore, if you want to personally experience this realm I have elucidated, you must penetrate thoroughly. It doesn't depend on sitting meditation or on clam-talk. What is this principle of the secret saying not concealed?

We could call it the indestructible immanent body;
That body is empty, clear, and luminous.

51

Rujing

Rujing studied with Zen master Zhijian. Zhijian asked him, "How can you purify what has never been defiled?" After more than a year Rujing was suddenly awakened and said, "I've hit upon that which is undefiled."

Rujing gave up doctrinal studies and went into Zen when he was nineteen years old. He joined the community of Zen master Zhijian and spent a year there constantly sitting in meditation, which he did more than the others. At one point, when he asked to be put in charge of cleaning the latrines, Zhijian asked him, "How can you clean what has never been dirty? If you can tell me, I'll put you in charge of cleaning." Rujing was at a loss; even after two or three months had passed he still didn't know what to say.

Once Zhijian called him to the abbot's room and asked him if he could say anything about this issue. Rujing hesitated. Zhijian said, "How can you purify what has never been defiled?" Rujing passed another year and more without being able to answer. Zhijian asked again, but Rujing couldn't give a reply. Then Zhijian said, "If you would get out of your old nest you would find a way. Why can't you say?" After that Rujing was strengthened and worked on meditation with determination.

One day Rujing was suddenly enlightened. He went to the abbot's quarters and said, "I can say it." Zhijian said, "This time say it." Rujing said, "I've hit upon that which is undefiled." Even before he finished speaking, Zhijian hit him. Rujing broke out in a sweat. Then he bowed, and Zhijian approved him.

Later, at another monastery, Rujing worked as the latrine cleaner, as a way of requiting the circumstances of his enlightenment. Once as he was passing in front of the shrine of saints, a strange monk there said to him, "Cleaner of the monastery, you requite the Way, you requite the Teacher, you requite the Community," and then disappeared. The prime minister of China heard about this and interpreted it to mean that the sages would approve of Rujing being abbot at that monastery. Later it actually turned out that way. People everywhere said that Rujing's virtue of requital was truly consummate.

After he made his determination at the age of nineteen, Rujing stayed in monasteries, never returning to his native place. Not only that, he didn't even talk to people from his homeland. He never visited any of the rooms of the monastery, and didn't even speak to those who sat by him in the monks' hall. He just sat. He vowed that he would sit through even a seat of diamond. Once his flesh became ulcerated from so much sitting, but he still didn't stop. From his first inspiration through his last abbacy there wasn't a single day or night that he didn't sit.

Throughout his abbacy at several public monasteries, Rujing's self-discipline was different from others, in that he was committed to being the same as the monks. Although he had the patchwork robe handed down from Zen master Daokai, therefore, he didn't wear it. During his lectures and individual guidance he just wore a black surplice and robe. Although he was given a purple vestment of honor and a master's title by the emperor of China, he formally declined them. Furthermore, he kept his succession a secret, not revealing it all his life; only at the end did he formally acknowledge the teacher from whom he had inherited the teaching. This was not only to put off worldly craving for fame, but also out of deference for the good name of Zen. Truly his virtue was unequaled in his time, his discipline peerless in ancient or modern times.

He used to declare of himself, "The Way of the Zen founders has died out this last century or two. Thus there has not appeared a teacher like me for the last hundred or two hundred years." Therefore the abbots in all quarters were awed by him. He never praised any of them. He used to say, "Since I made up my mind to go traveling at the age of nineteen, I have found no one imbued with the Way. Many of the monastery abbots just deal with visiting officials and pay no mind to the monks' hall. They always say, "Each of you should understand on your own," and so saying they do not develop the people. Even the abbots of great monasteries now are like this. They think having nothing on the mind is the Way, and don't demand intensive Zen concentration in association with a teacher. Where is there any Buddhism in that? If it is as they say, why would there be old-timers persistently seeking the Way? What a laugh—they haven't so much as dreamed of the Way of the Zen founders."

Among the many virtues of Rujing recorded in the diary of one of his attendants, it is said that he didn't say a word when a certain government official asked him to speak at the yamen, and he returned ten thousand pieces of silver that had been presented to him. When he didn't say anything, he not only did not accept the offerings of others, he did not accept fame or profit. So he didn't associate with rulers or politicians, and didn't even receive the greetings of traveling monks from various quarters.

Rujing's virtues were truly extraordinary. It was for this reason that a certain Taoist elder and five of his followers joined Rujing's community, pledging not to return to their native place without mastering Zen. Rujing was delighted at their determination and allowed them individual guidance without requiring them to formally convert to Buddhism. In the arrangement of the assembly he put them after the nuns. This was something quite unusual.

There was also someone named Shanru who vowed he would stay in Rujing's community all his life and never take a single step south. There were many who likewise determined never to leave the master's assembly. Pu the gardener was totally illiterate and didn't begin to study Zen until he was over sixty years old, but Rujing still developed him carefully, so that he finally became enlightened. Though he was a gardener, from time to time he used to utter extraordinary and marvelous sayings. Once Rujing said in a lecture that the abbots throughout the country were not equal to gardener Pu. Later Rujing assigned him to keep the library. Truly, in an assembly where there is the Way, there are many people imbued with the Way, many people with the heart of the Way.

Rujing always used to exhort people just to sit. He would say, "Burning incense, doing prostrations, reciting Buddha names, performing repentance ceremonies, and reciting scriptures are not needed—just sit." He only made them sit. He always said, "The beginning of Zen study is to have the heart of the Way." Truly, even if they have some knowledge or understanding, those who lack the heart of the Way cannot keep their understanding and eventually fall into erroneous views and become wild—they are outsiders sticking to Buddhism.

Therefore, good people, first of all don't forget the heart of the Way. Develop your mind fully, concentrate only on truth and don't follow the fashions of the time—go forward to emulate the Way of time immemorial.

In truth, if you are this way, even if you don't attain understanding you will be an originally undefiled person. If you are undefiled, this is being originally clean and pure. Thus: "There has never been defilement—what would you purify? If you can get out of your old nest you will find a way."

The teachings devised by the enlightened ones of old did not cause people to produce fragmentary knowledge and understanding—having them cultivate refining practice, setting their wills on the ultimate truth, they are without partiality. This is how one may at all times be free from the views of purity or defilement, and be undefiled oneself.

But so long as he still hadn't escaped the view of defilement, Rujing had an eye to use a means of cleaning: having passed more than a year without understanding, once he got so that there was no skin to strip off, no body or mind to shed, he said he had hit upon what has never been defiled. Yet even so, already he had a spot on him—that is why it says his teacher hit him even before he had finished speaking. At that point his whole body broke out in a sweat—having let go of his body, he attained power. So we know that original purity has never been subject to defilement at all. Therefore Rujing always used to say, "Zen study is the shedding of body and mind."

Now tell me, what is the undefiled?

The breeze of the Way, blowing far,
Is harder than diamond;
The whole earth is supported by it.

52

Dogen

Dogen studied with Zen master Rujing. Once during meditation sitting late at night Rujing said to the assembly, "Zen study is the shedding of mind and body." Hearing this, suddenly Dogen was greatly enlightened. He went right to the abbot's room and lit incense. Rujing asked him, "What are you burning incense for?" Dogen said, "My body and mind have been shed." Rujing said, "Body and mind shed, shed body and mind." Dogen said, "This is a temporary byway—don't approve me arbitrarily." Rujing said, "I'm not." Dogen said, "What is that which isn't given arbitrary approval?" Rujing said, "Shedding body and mind." Dogen bowed. Rujing said, "The shedding is shed."

At that time Rujing's attendant said, "This is no small matter, that a foreigner has attained such a state." Rujing said, "How many times has he been pummeled here—liberated, dignified, thunder roars."

Dogen was a ninth-generation descendant of Emperor Murakami. He was born in the year 1200. A physiognomist looked him over and said, "This child is an infant sage. His eyes have double pupils. He will surely be a great man. In an ancient book it says that when a sage is born among men, his mother is in danger. This child will surely lose his mother when he is seven years old." Hearing this, his mother was not disturbed or afraid. She loved and honored him all the more. And as it turned out, in his eighth year his mother died.

Everyone said that although there was a discrepancy of a year, after all it accorded with the physiognomist's statement.

In the winter of his fourth year, Dogen first learned to read Chinese poetry at his grandmother's knee. At the age of seven he presented his father with a collection of poems he had composed himself in Chinese. At that time all the elders and famous Confucian scholars declared him a prodigy.

When he lost his mother at the age of eight, Dogen's grief was most profound. As he watched the smoke of the incense rising at her funeral, he realized the transience of life, and from that point on he determined to seek enlightenment. In the spring of his ninth year he first read Vasubandhu's *Abhidharmakosha-shastra*. The old Buddhist priests said he was as bright as Manjusri, the embodiment of wisdom, and had genuine potential for universalist Buddhism. Dogen, mindful of such words even from youth, studied hard.

At that time Fujiwara Moroie, the regent and chief adviser to the emperor of Japan, a peerless model for rulers and ministers, took Dogen as an adopted son. He passed his secrets on to Dogen and taught him the essentials of political affairs. When Dogen was thirteen, the regent had him make his debut with the intention of having him become a courtier. Dogen, however, secretly left the manor and went to Mount Hiei, the center of the Tendai Buddhist school.

At that time there was a high priest named Ryokan, a master of the exoteric and esoteric teachings, who was also Dogen's maternal uncle. Dogen went to him and asked to be ordained as a monk. Ryokan was very much surprised. He asked, "But your elder brother and your foster father will be angry—what about that?" Dogen said, "When my mother was dying she told me to leave home and study the Way. And I also think I should do so—I don't want to be involved in the futilities of the mundane world. I just want to leave home and be a monk. I want to become a monk to requite my debt to my mother and grandmothers." Ryokan wept and took him in as a student.

At the age of fourteen Dogen finally had his head shaved, submitting to the authority of the high priest Koen. The next day he received the universalist precepts and became a monk. After that he learned the stopping and seeing practices of the Tendai school, as well as the esoteric teachings from southern India. By the time he was eighteen he had read the entire Buddhist canon.

Later Dogen went to the high priest Koin, another one of his uncles and an outstanding sage, to ask about the main issue of the religion. Koin told him, "What you are in doubt about is the ultimate point of our religion. This is something that has been passed on by word of mouth over the generations, since the time of the founder of the Tendai school. I cannot clear this doubt up for you. I have heard that a great master named Bodhidharma came from India to China transmitting the Buddha seal. His sect has now spread all over and is called the Zen school. If you want to settle this matter, go to the high priest Eisai at Kennin monastery and ask him about it, or go abroad to see the Way."

So in the fall of his eighteenth year Dogen joined the community of Eisai's successor Myozen at Kennin monastery and was initiated. When Eisai was the abbot at Kennin and Buddhist priests came to study with him, he would let them become Zen monks only after three years, but Dogen was permitted to don the garb of a Zen monk the same season. In late fall he was given the major robe and regarded as a vessel of the Way.

As for Myozen, he transmitted the three sects of exoteric, esoteric, and mind Buddhism. He was the designated successor of Eisai. In the annals of Kennin monastery it said, "The treasury of the teaching is entrusted to Myozen alone. Those who would seek the teaching of Eisai should ask of Myozen."

So Dogen studied with Myozen, from whom he again received the universalist precepts. He was given the robe and bowl symbolic of Zen tradition, and also received secret teachings of esoteric rituals. He studied the canon of monastic regulations as well, and also studied stopping and seeing. For the first time he heard about the way of Rinzai Zen, and, receiving the transmission of the true lineage of the three sects—exoteric, esoteric, and Zen—he became the sole heir of Myozen.

At the age of twenty-four, after about seven years of study with Myozen, Dogen left Kennin and headed for China. The first of the various teachers he visited in China was Rutan, who asked him, "When did you arrive here?" Dogen said, "Four months ago." Rutan said, "Did you come this way following a group?" Dogen said, "How is it when one comes thus, not following a group?" Rutan said, "This is still coming this way following a group." Dogen said, "Since this is coming thus following a group, what is right?" Rutan slapped him and said, "This talkative priest!" Dogen said, "Not that there is no talkative priest, but what is right?" Rutan said, "Stay for some tea."

Dogen also met master Sicho, whom he asked, "What is Buddha?" Sicho said, "The one in the shrine." Dogen said, "If it's the one in the shrine, how can it pervade the universe?" Sicho said, "Pervading the universe." Dogen said, "Fallen in words."

Having thus engaged in dialogue with various teachers, Dogen became very conceited and thought there was no one in Japan or China equal to himself. As he was about to head back to Japan, someone told him, "The only one in China with the eye of the Way is old Rujing—you will surely benefit by seeing him." Even so, it was over a year before he had the opportunity to call on Rujing.

At that time Zen master Rujing had just become abbot at a certain public monastery, replacing the recently deceased former abbot. Considering circumstances meet, Dogen went to him to resolve his doubts. At the very outset his attack was blunted, and hence he became a disciple of Rujing. Intending to complete his studies, he presented a letter saying, "I have set my heart on enlightenment since youth, and though I have sought the Way from various teachers in my own country and came to know something of the basis of cause and effect, I still didn't know the ultimate goal of Buddhism and lingered in the understanding of the externals of names and forms. Later I entered the room of Zen master Eisai and first heard the way of Rinzai Zen. Now I have come to China with master Myozen, and have gotten the opportunity to join your congregation. This is the luck of a past blessing. Now I pray that in your great compassion you will allow a foreigner, an insignificant man from a distant place, to freely come to your room to ask about the teaching, without question of time or manner. Please be so merciful and kind as to permit me this." Rujing permitted Dogen to call on him day or night, saying he would be like a father forgiving his son's lack of manners.

After that Dogen met with the teacher day and night, personally receiving the true secret. At one point Dogen was chosen to be one of the teacher's attendants, but he declined, saying, "I am a foreigner; if I were to become an attendant in a major monastery of this great country, there would be a lot of suspicion and criticism in the monastic community. I only want to meet with the teacher morning and night." The teacher said, "What you say is truly humble and not without reason." So he just engaged in dialogue with the teacher and received instruction.

Then one night during sitting meditation in the latter part of the night, Rujing came into the hall and admonished the group for sleeping, saying, "Zen study is a matter of shedding body and mind. It does not require incense burning, prostrations, recitations of Buddha names, repentance ceremonies, or scripture reading. You accomplish it by just sitting." Hearing this, Dogen was suddenly enlightened.

Since the time he met Rujing, Dogen worked on the Way day and night, never slacking off for a moment. Therefore he never lay down. Rujing used to say to him, "You have the discipline of the ancient Buddhas—you will surely spread the Way of Zen. My finding you is like Shakyamuni Buddha finding Kasyapa." So in 1225 Dogen was formally recognized as a successor to the teaching. Rujing instructed him, "Return to your native country and spread the Zen Way. Live in obscurity deep in the mountains and mature your enlightenment."

Dogen also saw succession documents of the five schools of Zen while he was in China. At first he met Zen master Weiyi, who told him, "Ancient writings worth seeing are valuable treasures for people. How many have you seen?" Dogen said he hadn't seen any, so Weiyi told him he had one he would show him. When he brought it out it turned out to be a succession document of the Fayan lineage. It was not his own; Weiyi said that he had found it among the effects of an old adept.

Later the chief monk at the monastery where Dogen studied under Rujing showed him a succession document from the Yunmen lineage. Dogen asked him, "Why are there differences among the five schools of Zen? If the succession is continuous from India to China, how could there be differences?" He said, "Even if the differences are enormous, you should just learn that the Buddhism of Yunmen is thus. Why is Shakyamuni Buddha respected? Because he was enlightened. Why is Zen master Yunmen respected? Because he was enlightened." From this Dogen got some perspective on the matter.

There was also a librarian who had a succession document that he showed to a Japanese monk who had taken care of him when he was sick, saying, "This is something difficult to get to see, but I will let you look at it." Six months later, that Japanese monk entreated the librarian to show it to Dogen also; it was a succession document of the Yangqi lineage of the Linji school of Zen. Dogen also saw the succession documents of two other Zen masters.

Thus having received the permission of several teachers and gotten Rujing's recognition, having mastered the great concern of a lifetime and received the teachings of the Zen founders, Dogen returned to Japan in 1227.

After that Dogen looked for a beautiful place to live unobtrusively. He looked over thirteen places offered by patrons, but none of them suited him. He stayed for some time at a temple on the outskirts of the ancient capital of Kyoto; by then he was thirty-four years old. Monks gradually gathered, seeking the Way, eventually numbering over fifty. Ten years later he moved to the remote countryside and founded what is now Eihei monastery deep in the mountains.

To penetrate Zen, first one must clarify the mind. In the story of Dogen's enlightenment, we hear that Zen study is the shedding of body and mind. In truth, in Zen study we must relinquish attachments to body and mind. If one is not yet free from body and mind, it is not the Way. It is thought that the body is skin, flesh, bones, and marrow, but when you perceive minutely you cannot apprehend the slightest substance.

The mind as spoken of here is of two kinds. One is thinking and discriminating; this perceiving and distinguishing consciousness is thought to be the mind. The second is silent and still, with no knowledge or understanding; here the profound stillness of spiritual brightness is thought to be the mind. What people don't realize is that this is still the root of discriminating consciousness. The ancients called this the place where the spiritual brightness is unmoving. Don't dwell in this, thinking it to be mind.

When we see in detail, there is a threefold distinction: mind, cognition, and consciousness. "Consciousness" is the mind that likes and dislikes, affirms and denies, approves and disapproves. "Cognition" discerns distinctions such as coolness and warmth, pain and itch. "Mind" does not distinguish right or wrong, or feel pain or itch; it is like a wall, like a stone. You think this is really still and silent; it is as though this mind had no ears or eyes. Therefore when speaking on the basis of this "mind" one is like a wood or iron mannikin; though having eyes you don't see, though having ears you don't hear. At this point no words or ideas can convey it. Though this state is mind, yet this is the seed of awareness of distinctions. Cognition and consciousness are based on this, so don't consider it the original mind.

We say that study of the Way must be apart from mind, cognition, and consciousness: these are not to be thought of as the body-mind. There is beyond this a single spiritual light that is eternal and stable. If you observe carefully and thoroughly you will surely reach it. If you can clarify the mind, there is no body or mind to be found, no things or self accompanying it. This is why it is said that body and mind are shed.

Reaching this point, when you observe closely, even if you use a thousand eyes you do not find a particle of anything that can be called skin, flesh, bones, or marrow; there is nothing to divide into mind, cognition, and consciousness. How can you know coolness and warmth, how can you distinguish pain and itch? What would you affirm or deny, what like or dislike? Therefore it has been said, "When you see, there is not a single thing." Having reached this point, Dogen expressed it by saying he had shed body and mind. Rujing then acknowledged him, saying, "Body and mind shed, shed body and mind." And finally he said, "Shedding is shed."

Once having reached this state, one will be like a bottomless basket, like a perforated cup—no matter how much you put into it, it is never filled. Reaching this is called "the bottom falling out of the bucket." If you have any thought at all of having some enlightenment or attainment, it is not the Way—it will just be a livelihood of exercising the spirit.

Comprehend thoroughly, investigate and penetrate completely, and you will know there is a body that has no skin, flesh, bones, or marrow. This body cannot be shed even though one try to shed it; it cannot be abandoned even though one try to abandon it. Therefore this realm is referred to by the expression, "When all is exhausted, there is a place that cannot be emptied."

If you can understand thoroughly, you won't doubt what the Zen masters and Buddhas say. What is this principle?

Clear as pure light, no inside or outside—
Is there any body or mind to be shed?

53

Ejo

Ejo studied with Zen master Dogen. One day in the course of inquiries he heard the saying, "One hair goes through myriad holes," and all of a sudden realized enlightenment. That evening he went to Dogen and said, "I do not ask about the one hair—what about the myriad holes?" Dogen smiled and said, "Gone through." Ejo bowed.

Ejo was from a noble family. He became a monk at the age of eighteen, under the tutelage of a high priest. He studied elementary Buddhist philosophy, then learned the methods of stopping and seeing according to the Tendai school of Buddhism. In the course of his study he realized that it is worthless to learn Buddhism for the sake of honor and gain. Within himself he conceived the determination for enlightenment, although for the time being he followed his teacher's will and worked at formal studies for the sake of progress.

Once when he went to his mother's place, she said to him, "My intention in having you leave home was not that you would have a high rank and mix with the nobles, but that you would refrain from studying for the sake of fame and profit and become a black-robed outcaste with your rain hat behind your back, just going along on your travels."

Ejo agreed. He changed his vestments and never went back to Mount Hiei, the Tendai center. He then studied the teachings of the Pure Land school. Later he went to Kakuen, a Zen master preaching the doctrine of seeing essence, and studied more energetically and thoroughly than all the others there.

Once there was a discussion of the Heroic March Scripture. Coming to the point where it says in the metaphor of the pot that the emptiness inside the pot cannot be increased by adding emptiness or decreased by taking emptiness away, Ejo had a profound realization. Kakuen said, "How could it be that the roots of evil and the barriers of confusion that have been there since beginningless time have all melted away and you have become completely liberated from all pain and misery!" At that time there were more than thirty students in the group; they all thought Ejo most remarkable, and all paid respect to him.

In 1227, when Zen master Dogen had just come back from China, he was staying in Kennin monastery refining his practice. At that time it was said that he had brought the true teaching from China and inwardly intended to spread it. Hearing of this, Ejo thought to himself, "I already have some realization of the source of the three kinds of stopping and three kinds of seeing taught in the Tendai school, and I have mastered the essential practice of the Pure Land teaching. What is more, I have studied with Kakuen and have a profound realization of the meaning of seeing essence and realizing buddhahood. What could it be that this Dogen has brought?"

To find out, Ejo went and called on Dogen. When they first talked, for two or three days Dogen's understanding was just the same as Ejo's; they talked about the spiritual knowledge of seeing natural reality, and Ejo happily concurred, all the more respectful because of his feeling that his own attainment was genuine. But after several days Dogen revealed some very unusual understanding. Ejo was startled, but as he began to challenge Dogen, he found that Dogen had a truth quite different from and beyond his own.

Thus Ejo's inspiration was renewed, and he sought to study with Dogen. Dogen told him, "I am transmitting the source teaching and want to spread it in Japan. Although I may as well stay here in Kennin for the time being, I want to find another place to live. If I find a place and build a hut, then you should come see me. It is not suitable for you to follow me here in this monastery." So Ejo awaited the proper time, in accord with Dogen's will.

Later Dogen built a hermitage next to a temple on the outskirts of Kyoto and lived there alone. For two years not a single person came, until Ejo showed up in 1234. Dogen gladly allowed Ejo to receive personal guidance, discussing the Way of Zen day and night. After three years, Dogen brought up the saying about one hair passing through myriad holes. That is to say, "One instant is ten thousand years; one hair goes through myriad holes. To pass the test is up to you; to surpass the crowd is up to you." Hearing this, Ejo became enlightened. After receiving Dogen's acknowledgment and approval, Ejo followed him continuously for twenty years, never leaving his presence even for a day, like a shadow following a form.

No matter what other job Ejo held, he always served as Dogen's attendant as well. When his tasks were done, he would go back to the attendants' quarters and stay there. Therefore I always used to hear Ejo say, "Although Myozen had numerous disciples, only master Dogen finished his studies there; and while Dogen had many disciples, I walked alone in the abbot's room. Therefore I heard things others did not hear, while there was nothing others heard that I did not."

After he became the successor of the school, Ejo was always highly esteemed by Dogen, who had him take charge of all the Buddhist services at Eihei monastery. When Ejo asked him the reason, Dogen said, "I will not live very long, and you will outlive me; it will certainly be you who will cause the Way to spread. Therefore I esteem you for the sake of the teaching."

Dogen's attitude toward Ejo was almost like that of a student to a teacher. The paths of teacher and apprentice joined, the lights of their minds and eyes merging, like water in water, like space meeting space. With no disagreement at all between them, only Ejo knew the mind of Dogen, which was beyond the knowledge of others.

As for the meaning of "one hair going through myriad holes," Ejo said, "I don't ask about the one hair—what about the myriad holes?" There is not so much as a single atom that can be established;

nothing can be produced at all. Therefore an ancient said, "In the sphere of true reality not so much as a single atom can be accommodated." In the single expanse of pure emptiness, nothing so much as a fine hair is produced. When Ejo had understood in this way, Dogen approved of him by saying, "Gone through." Actually hundreds of thousands of inconceivable meanings and infinite avenues of teaching were all strung on a single hair. Ultimately there is not a mote of dust that comes from outside.

So there are no boundaries in the ten directions, no differences in the past, present, and future. Crystal clear, bright and radiant, this realm is even brighter than a thousand suns shining together—even if a thousand eyes looked it over, they couldn't find its limits. Yet no one doubts that it is clearly comprehended when one is awakened; therefore it is not something extinct. It is not of the character of distinction; it has no movement, no stillness, no hearing, no seeing. Have you reached it in every way, thoroughly realized it in this way?

If you haven't attained this point, even if you practice virtuously for tens of thousands of years and meet innumerable Buddhas, this is all fabricated practice, and you do not understand anything about the Way of Zen. Therefore you cannot avoid the miserable routines of the three realms and will not cut off the flow of birth in its various forms.

If you formally model yourselves on the Buddha and make use of the endowment of the Buddha but have no realization of the Buddha's enlightened mind, you are not only deceiving yourselves at all times, but are also repudiating the Buddhas. Therefore you cannot destroy the ground of ignorance and wander around in the cluster of habitual consciousness. Even if you experience states of felicity by the power of virtue and proudly enjoy this conditional happiness, this is just like the wheel of a cart that sometimes goes through wet places and sometimes goes through dry places—endlessly, beginninglessly, you will just be sentient beings experiencing the results of habitual action.

So even if you have mastered the canonical teachings of Buddhism and can expound their doctrines, this is after all just like a cat watching a rat—even though you outwardly seem to be quiet, your

mind is still restlessly seeking. And even if your cultivation of practice is closely refined, your mind ground is never really tranquil, and
so your doubts and hesitations are not yet cleared up. This is like a fox
that runs fast yet makes slow progess because it keeps looking back.
This is a life of playing with the spirit, the life of a foxy devil whose
changing apparition has not ceased.

Therefore you should not be fond of academic learning. All you
should do is arouse your will for the moment, even for an instant, so
that it is like a great fire in which nothing can remain, like open space
to which nothing can be affixed. Then even if you think, you will definitely reach the point where thought cannot reach; and even if you
don't think, you will definitely reach the point that cannot be emptied. If you have such a true determination, once this will is solidified
you will penetrate through to a realization no different from that of
the Buddhas of all times.

Dogen said, "When people seek the Way, they should do so with
the same determination as worldly people have when they seek to
meet a beauty, to overcome a powerful adversary, or to conquer a
fortified citadel. Once they have such a profound determination,
they will surely overcome this adversary, meet this beauty, or conquer this citadel. Now if you apply this mind to the Way, everyone
should attain enlightenment." The Way is the formless teaching of
universalist Buddhism. You should not think that it necessarily
makes a distinction among potentialities, or that beginners cannot
reach it. Here there is no sharpness or dullness at all; there is nothing
whatsoever to work at. Burst forth once, and you should have profound realization.

Now tell me, what is this principle? I have already told you: space
has never admitted so much as a needle, in the vastness there is nothing to rely on—who is there to discuss it? When you arrive at this
realm, you do not establish even the name of a single hair, much less
the myriad holes. Nevertheless, there is something that myriad
things cannot hide, and even when everything is done away with,
there is still something you cannot get rid of. It stands out clearly of
itself; empty and open, it is fundamentally radiantly aware. Therefore it is called "clean and naked, bare and free." It is also called being

clearly awake, everything obvious; and it is called radiant brightness. There is not a trace of doubt or thought, nor any floating dust at all. It is brighter even than a billion suns and moons.

But you cannot call it white, you cannot call it red. It is like waking up from a dream—it is only alive and active. We call this living: to be awake means having awakened and being alert; being clear means being bright and lucid. You should not say that there is no inside or outside, you should not say that it extends through the past or reaches the present. So do not say that one hair goes through myriad holes—what going through could there be? If you call it a hair, this is what Ejo already realized; then what is the substance of the hair?

> Space has never admitted even a needle;
> In the vastness there is nothing to rely on,
> So who is there to discuss it?
> Do not say one hair goes through myriad holes—
> The bare, clean ground hasn't a trace.

Design by David Bullen
Typeset in Mergenthaler Bembo
with Centaur display
by Wilsted & Taylor
Printed by Maple-Vail
on acid-free paper